We Tried to Warn You

Innovations in leadership for the learning organization

Innovation, Product Management, Strategic Foresight, and Learning from Failure

Engineers warned NASA that liftoff damage could be dangerous before the loss of space shuttle Columbia. This photo shows the hangar where the ship was reassembled.

Peter H. Jones

NIMBLE BOOKS LLC

ISBN-13: 978-1-934840-51-1

ISBN-10: 1-934840-51-3

Copyright 2008 Peter H. Jones

Last saved 2009-07-23.

Nimble Books LLC

1521 Martha Avenue

Ann Arbor, MI 48103-5333

http://www.nimblebooks.com

Illustrations © 2008 Peter H. Jones. Cover photograph by NASA.

This book was produced using Microsoft Word 2007 and Adobe Acrobat 8.1. The cover was produced using The Gimp. The cover font, heading fonts and the body text inside the book are in Constantia, designed by John Hudson for Microsoft.

Contents

Introduction iv
Buy This Book If: v
About the Author vi
Acknowledgments vii
We Win and Lose, Together 1
    Organizations as Wicked Problems 4
Navigating the Product Organization 12
    Decisions across Organizational Structure 14
    Project Dynamics and Failure Mechanisms 17
    Participating in Innovation 21
    The Power of Customer Evidence 24
    Influencing and Learning Opportunities 26
    Integrating the Multidisciplinary Organization 28
Lateral Leadership across Boundaries 32
    Organic Growth - by Drift and by Design 33
    Organizational Process Socialization 37
    Organizations as Self-Protection Systems 40
    Innovation Sensing and Organizational Learning 42
Adaptive Organizational Design 45
    Co-Creating an Iterative Organization 48
Conclusions 56
Bibliography 59
Letter from the Publisher 61

INTRODUCTION

This book was written as a response to the positive and heartening reception to a series of articles published (online and print) on innovative interventions in organizations. The core message of *We Tried to Warn You* is that failures happen, often resulting from poor communications and the lack of foresight, and that the lateral leadership of people working across boundaries repairs and prevents organizational failures. I report on first-hand experiences as a participant, and more recently as a design/management consultant, also informed by research.

The book title draws from the spirit of the front lines of work, where a broken strategy is often recognized long before management. The people working closest to the customers are able to foresee the potential for disconnects among a product's strategy, its design, and the user's adoption. What we may later call a strategic breakdown was foreseeable and perhaps repairable. Those working with users and customers are able to make sense of direct behavioral observations and connect these to the company's future prospects. Senior managers may ignore this source of insight, since it does not originate from their acknowledged credible communication channels. *We Tried to Warn You* may appear to celebrate the knowing *schadenfreude* of those in customer-facing positions, who may have some stake in the current world. However, this attitude is only the first, dramatic impulse we see when the concerns of user-oriented employees (sales, marketing, or product development) are ignored and then later become obvious in widely-shared reality. When an organization creates a new atmosphere that encourages shared, lateral leadership, the separation between front lines and management tends to blur and organizational communication improves, largely by virtue of the network effect and the perceived importance of sensing from the front lines.

I present such a case study in compact form, with identifying details obscured to protect real organizations and their employees. I focus emphasis on the *knowledge practices* that enable organizations to sense and make decisions from critical feedback from customers in the field. While the case presents a situation emerging from the multidisciplinary field now known as user experience design (UX), a similar story could be about the development and diffusion of other knowledge-based practices in organizations. A core theme of *We Tried to Warn You* is that knowledge must be located, translated, and mobilized from the front lines back to the business in creative communications, informing product strategy and innovation. The user experience group permits a perfect case study, as in many companies it has now become a primary conduit for understanding "real users" and their needs in current organizations worldwide. The user experience group is also involved throughout all phases of product innovation, from user research, to product concept design, to final design and user testing.

In the case study, new skills and job roles were developed in this organization as a response to a systemic failure, with outstanding positive results. The book shares these lessons learned from a process we call *socializing*, which, like the new hire "onboarding" process also known as socialization, refers to the development of lateral relationships in leadership. Socialization is an organizational process that intentionally distributes leadership and skill development across boundaries and among organizational players in the formation of key strategic functions such as User Experience, Innovation, Research and Development, Market Research, or Knowledge Management. These functions all translate knowledge from original sources to the nerve centers of the business, and have unique skill sets with much to offer to all projects in a contemporary products or services firm.

BUY THIS BOOK IF:

- You are interested in improving organizational foresight, internal knowledge of customer behaviors, and the hidden talents of leadership among everyone in your company.
- You see the possibility for everyone in your company to improve communications and leadership. And you are ready to start with yourself.
- You want to nip failures in the bud in your own company. Learning to break unwanted news before it becomes really bad news later is a gift that takes courage, acuity, and wisdom.
- You have ever ever been on a large project that failed or almost failed in the marketplace, and you wondered how smart people in hard-working organizations can overlook the issues that lead to problems.
- You sense a larger vision for success is possible at all companies, from start-up to mega. This success may mean building a winning product platform, working with the best people in a winning company, and integrating product and business strategy around your actual users.
- You are willing to take responsibility for improving your organization.

About the Author

Peter Jones lives and works in both the US and Canada. An experienced design research and strategy consultant, he founded Redesign Research in 2001. Redesign Research specializes in depth research for human-centered innovation. Peter has designed market-leading interactive information services for legal, medical, business, and scientific applications.

He completed his Ph.D. in Design and Innovation Management) at The Union Institute. Peter conducts and publishes research on organizational innovation, collaborative knowledge creation, organizational and knowledge strategy, and social and participatory technologies (such as dialogue and networks). His scholarly research agenda investigates how professionals use information in their decision-making, how people knowledge practices are formed, and how organizational values are formed and affect products and business performance.

His current management research explores ways in which organizations might design practices of long-range foresight and reflective renewal to improve innovation. This research expresses a perspective on organizational transformation based on fundamental revisioning of strategies aligned with values. Based on such research, Peter advocates (in this book) an approach of process socialization of new organizational styles and practices to accelerate innovation, enhance everyday work, and promote values leadership.

Peter is founding partner of Dialogic Design International, a boutique consultancy that advances the use of structured dialogue for democratic engagement of stakeholders in navigating complex problems in technology and strategic sectors. He is also board member of the Institute for 21st Century Agoras, a non-profit with similar aims of facilitating stakeholder collaboration in social and civil sectors.

Peter wrote *Team Design: A Practitioner's Guide to Collaborative Innovation* in 1998, and revised it in 2002. Many of his articles can be found online. He posts a blog at designdialogues.com.

ACKNOWLEDGMENTS

I acknowledge my mother Betsy, who instilled in me a love of reading, writing, and art, as well as the meaning of contribution in your communities. I also thank my father Hayward, who has supported me throughout a life of learning. Their wisdom is with me, somewhere, every day. Thanks to Patricia Kambitsch, who read and complimented the book as the most readable piece I've written to date (so it must be good). This means a lot, since Patricia is the best – and funniest - author I know. She is also my wife and partner in many projects.

Many thanks to Nimble Books publisher Fred Zimmerman for collaborating on the project, and transforming my writing into book form. This book, and the series of books we envision for *Designing Organizations that Matter*, would never have happened without his guidance and interest.

WE WIN AND LOSE, TOGETHER

Failures constantly occur in large, complex business organizations. Taking a straightforward definition of failure as "something that falls short of what is required or expected," they are constant. Every day, breakdowns happen at every level of interaction, from the strategic to the interpersonal. Some of these are prosaic and even helpful, allowing us to safely and iteratively learn and improve communications and practices. We tend to fix everyday mistakes and move on, and may not assign the pejorative "failure" to these situations unless the consequences are unusually severe.

Organizations are resilient and redundant by structure. We should therefore consider everyday "micro" failures as considered valuable learning opportunities. Everybody makes mistakes, and people learn best when applying their skills and having freedom to make mistakes. Even poorly managed projects are recoverable. Typically direct labor employees understand their shared responsibility for success and compensate for the poor performance of others, regardless of weak oversight.

Other failures are systemic and large-scale, and can wreak havoc for years. We have recently witnessed the implosion of major financial institutions following the collapse of credit and the housing market bubble in 2008. Like a crumbling foundation, systemic failures may not show until future stressors tip over the entire structure from within. These "macro" failures result from accumulated bad decisions, organizational defensiveness, and embedded organizational values that prevent people from confronting issues as they occur. Macro failures often start as poor communications patterns, are sustained by organizational values conflicts, and may end in reorganization and cynical blame-shifting. Even though this book's example is based on the simpler case of a retail computer systems firm losing a new strategic product line, the organizational dynamics and defenses are similar to those that occur in other industries. People in organizations behave in similar ways, and we can learn from one another's examples. Even if it is too late to advise Lehman Brothers, AIG, or Fannie Mae, we know now that these organizations had sufficient advance notice. They were warned from within and from without. Following the rapid failure of these institutions, reports were published that numerous warnings were communicated, within a reasonable time horizon for action, and from credible organizational agents such as Chief Risk Officers. We must recognize that collective defensiveness and wishful thinking draw from the same well across industries and firms.

Most of us experience anxiety when acknowledging personal responsibility for an everyday mistake. Consider, then, the inconceivable audacity required for a single person to stop the train of a massive organization-wide collapse of a project or product. Consider the improbability of making a difference. Once a systemic failure has gained the momentum of certainty, the company's fortunes can be seen riding on each decision. Leaders do not typically reveal their "integrity moments" freely during these breakdowns. When management avoids accountability for major failures, organizational learning is impeded at all levels, and future failures remain likely. During the chaos of unexpected organizational change, people are disinclined to reflect and learn. Once compelled by events into an emergency state, people follow a collective mood and keep their heads down. Given the sheer *scale* of such a breakdown, people avoid owning their role in the mess. Similar failures could happen again to these same firms.

We all have a role to play in detecting, anticipating, and confronting the decisions that lead to breakdowns that threaten the organization's standing. I believe many macro failures can be avoided if leaders pay attention to feedback, not from their pampered in-house executive councils, but from their end customers or "end users" of the products and services at the starting point of the value chain. *Customers* do not tilt reality toward our preferred direction; they have their own lives, interests, and opportunities that our services merely touch from time to time.

Most large product or service providers conduct market research in attempt to understand larger trends to guide marketing decisions. If we aim to align product strategies to aggregate customer responses, we must realize market research is a *lagging* trend indicator, it does not forecast future market behaviors. Surveys and focus groups are typically planned by product management to address very specific internal product decisions. Studies are often defensively constructed and narrowly focused, insensitive to the variations of reality, and often at the wrong level of resolution. They focus on features and pre-conceived consumer values, not on discovering actual behaviors and changes in trend or mood.

End users, the final stakeholders in the product value chain, may offer a stronger lead to foresight and a firm's best future responses to a changing market of "users." Observations drawn directly from encounters in field, by research design rather than anecdote, provide a much richer set of ideas and alternatives for a strategy when planning for those responses. Many organizations have no established process for tapping directly into end customer behavior, and they fail to capitalize on this always-available knowledge channel. We examine how we might tap into the real experiences of end customers for innovation guidance and an "early warning system" for products, marketing, business models and strategy.

To navigate the rapid change and complexity in today's wired markets, we can create continuous early innovation and early warning systems. A new organizational role is now possible, whose job is paying attention to weak signals and articulating insights to both suggest innovations and tactfully frame the bad news from the field. Currently some firms fulfill these roles are in the emerging and evolving capacities of "user experience." User experience (as defined by the interprofessional society UXNet.org) is defined as "the quality of experience a person has when interacting with a specific design. This can range from a specific artifact, such as a cup, toy or website, up to larger, integrated experiences such as a museum or an airport." The practice of "UX" has grown to embrace a collection of disciplines, including human factors, information and interaction design, usability, anthropology, and design strategy. It can be all of these or none, depending on the organization. To be effective, user experience design must attend closely to the real world of the customer. UX processes must be necessarily integrated into larger organizational decisions, and customer insights must become a type of *business intelligence*, and not merely remain a product of user experience. The customer knowledge summarized from Customer Service operations should be treated as business intelligence. These are critical functions of an innovation sensing system.

A dozen years ago innovations in "customer sensing" were called Voice of the Customer or Customer Advisory Boards. These organizational practices have the tendency to attract high-profile or special customers, usually executives only, tended to by specialized management. We have a responsibility to detect and assess the potential for product and strategic failure. We must try to stop the train, even if we are many steps removed from the decision making process at the root of these failures.

ORGANIZATIONS AS WICKED PROBLEMS

Consider the following case: Marketline (not their real name), a $2B market leader in retail store management computer systems, spends most of a decade developing its next-generation platform and product, and spends untold amounts in labor, licenses, contracting, testing, sales and marketing, and facilities. Due to the inherent complexity of the possible customer configurations, the project takes much longer than planned. Three technology waves come and go over the years, but are accommodated in an aggressive development strategy. The company's flagship product, a keyboard entry, terminal-based system running a 1980's era database server, continued to hold its market share while the replacement was in development, under deep cover. By the time web services technologies matured the new product emerged as a Windows NT server, networked application, with a "rich client" graphical user interface.

The product was designed to embody the current industry as well as best practices recommended by (major) customers. However, the structure of these best practices prevented the flexible configurations necessary for the customer base, and the platform performance compared poorly to the current product the new product was designed to replace. Users on the front lines of the customer stores rejected the system early in trial installations. Most stores never even gave it a chance. The well-planned, best-practices product became a huge write-off, wiping out most of a decade's worth of investment.

Marketline recovered by successfully face-lifting its existing, aging product to embrace contemporary user interface design standards. However, the company never developed a true replacement product. We return to this case study as an example of how organizations reinforce the wrong things. If the wrong product is built in the first place, it can never be "enhanced" to be the right product for the market. It may be better to enhance an older product with a continuous user base.

Other macro failure examples are easy to find when you know what kinds of evidence point to the initial failure. Most business or product failures are explained by "retrospective sensemaking." People trace events back in time from the inflection point when failure was obvious, as an exercise in (Karl Weick's[1]) *sensemaking*, which are "accounts that are socially acceptable and credible." A key notion in sensemaking is that people in organizations see only what they have beliefs to understand, and ignore or disbelieve situations for which they have no prior beliefs. Furthermore, beliefs (views of reality) and values (shared priorities and norms) are not readily changed even after the inevitable has happened. Sensemaking shows up in shared experience, but does not result in shared meaning. In other words, people in a situation (or "crisis") share an experience together, but have few ways of creating and distributing shared meaning across the organization. People tell stories in retrospect, and make joint sense of the crisis situation only later. In the moment of decision, when shared sensemaking could be most helpful, members usually have no organizational practices or rituals for organizing their communication and storytelling in a meaning-making way. They act on what they know, and "make sense" of the situation often much later in time. These are common, but plainly ineffective organizational learning behaviors.

People simplify and filter, and pull a story together when others, such as shareholders, demand an explanation. Executives, as storytellers, do not go for nuance and analysis. Leaders gain credibility from action and implementing. So the organization moves, as they say, "forward."

Macro organizational failures may be more common than we know, since they are covered up by board memos, press releases, and changes to strategy. Large firms appear to have an inherent, self-protecting blindness to failure dynamics as events unfold. They bury their massive mistakes. As Michael Raynor discussed in *The Strategy Paradox* (2007), our understanding of the performance of business strategies is all based on going firms. We have no way of knowing about the strategies of failed businesses (except as with Enron, those spectacular enough to make popular news), because they do not publish case studies about the decisions, causes, and history of their collapse. Raynor investigates and decides that many organizations have failed following "perfect" business strategies, typically extreme differentiation or extreme value pricing.

---

[1] Karl Weick, *Sensemaking in Organizations*, London: Sage Publications (1995).

From an organizational strategy and design perspective, several questions should be explored:

- What were the triggering mistakes or overlooked decisions that incrementally led to failure?
- At what point in these projects could anyone in the firm have predicted product adoption failure?
- How did designers contribute to the problem? What could product designers (e.g., user experience) have done instead?
- Were designers able to detect the problems that led to failure? Were they able to effectively project this and make a case based on foreseen risks?
- If people acted rationally and made apparently sound decisions, where did failures actually happen?
- What customer or user information did these case organizations have available to them? How did they interpret unwanted evidence?
- At what point was the product's failure in the market seen as inevitable? Is it possible to discern a tipping point?

Marketline's situation was not a failure of application design; it was a systemic failure with its roots in organizational communication. It appears to be a fairly common situation, and preventable. Obviously the market outcome was not the actual failure point. At the product's judgment day, the organization must recognize failure when its strategic goals fail with customers. So if this is the case, where did the failures occur?

It may be impossible to see whether and where failures will occur, for many reasons. People are generally unable to predict the systemic outcomes of situational actions; for example, product managers cannot trace the impact of an interface design issue to a failure of product adoption. Customers often use global language such as "ease of use" to describe a problem, rather than specific interaction problems. As a result, it can be very difficult to parse out the specific features that are responsible for the global concerns. People are also very bad at forecasting in general, or predicting improbable events. Failures are especially difficult to acknowledge, due to an organizational bias against recognizing that an event represents a failure.

Organizational actors are often unwilling to confront *small* breakdowns when they have occurred, let alone macro failures. For many leaders, acknowledging failures is a violation of beliefs. Business leaders may have unreasonably optimistic expectations for market performance, clouding their willingness to deal with emergent risks. When management teams plan to invest in a large program with the scale of new product development, they will have made informed judgments of the size of the market and the pace of sales and profits. Once planners have pitched a case and executives supported it, the revenue numbers can appear like self-fulfilling prophecies. They are etched in the plan, they must be true. Internal support leads to a positive bias.

We generally have a strong bias toward attributing our own skill when things go well and to assigning external contingencies when things go badly. As Taleb recounts in *The Black Swan*:

> *"We humans are the victims of an asymmetry in the perception of random events. We attribute our success to our skills, and our failures to external events outside our control, namely to randomness. We feel responsible for the good stuff, but not for the bad. This causes us to think that we are better than others at whatever we do for a living. Ninety-four percent of Swedes believe that their driving skills put them in the top 50 percent of Swedish drivers; 84 percent of Frenchmen feel that their lovemaking abilities put them in the top half of French lovers." (p. 152).*

Organizations are complex, self-organizing, socio-technical systems. In their complexity, modern organizations can be considered "wicked problems." Wicked problems call for approaches known as "design thinking;" they can be designed-to, but not necessarily designed. They cannot be "solved," at least not using the analytical approaches of so-called rational decision makers. Rittel and Webber identify 10 characteristics of a wicked problem.

1. There is no definite formulation of a wicked problem.
2. Wicked problems have no stopping rules (you don't know when you're done).
3. Solutions to wicked problems are not true-or-false, but better or worse.
4. There is no immediate or ultimate test of a solution to a wicked problem.
5. Every solution to a wicked problem is a "one-shot operation;" because there is no opportunity to learn by trial-and-error, every attempt counts significantly.
6. Wicked problems do not have an enumerable set of potential solutions.
7. Every wicked problem is essentially unique.
8. Every wicked problem can be considered to be a symptom of another [wicked] problem.
9. The causes of a wicked problem can be explained in many ways.
10. The planner has no right to be wrong.

Large organizations are and can be viewed as complex, dynamic social systems, having potentially many wicked problems occurring simultaneously. These attributes apply to both well-functioning and to failing organizations; in the case of those pitched in the chaos of product or planning failures, the wicked problem frame may appear unhelpful. One finds no easy way out of the mess, but yet conventional problem solving remains insufficient.

The wicked problem frame also helps explain why we cannot trace a series of decisions to the outcomes of failure —there are too many alternative options or explanations within such a complex field. Considering failure as a constant risk in a wicked problem scenario may instead offer a better way to think through the mess (as a design problem). However, there will be no way to trace back or even learn from the originating events that the organization might have caught early enough to prevent the massive failure chain. Too many different cascades will have occurred from each perturbation and each subsequent event. In a similar way, in the financial services industry, we have witnessed the phenomenon of "de-leveraging." When parties in a series of complex deals require liquidity or lose trust, demanding access to the underlying asset, the chain of "packaging" falls apart. Any chain of decisions can become far removed from an originating response or communication. When so-called Black Swan events[2] do occur, leaders make the claim that the event was unforeseeable. In all the recently published business or institutional failures stemming from the financial services / credit crisis (from 2003 – 2008), external observers, without access to inside information, predicted clearly and publicly that the accumulation of risk exposures would result in an imminent failure. Only insiders behave as if failure were not an option.

Therefore, we should view failure as an organizational dynamic, a process, not an event. By the time the signal failure event occurs (product adoption failure in intended market); the organizational failure is ancient history. Given the inherent complexity of large organizations, the dynamics of markets and timing products to market needs, and the interactions of hundreds of people in large projects, where do we start to look for the first cracks of large-scale failure?

Resilience vs. Adaptability

Must the failure of a product line organization (the smallest unit of analysis) threaten the viability of the company? An organizational-level failure is a recognizable event, one that typically follows a series of antecedent events or decisions that led to the large-scale breakdown. My working definition follows as:

> *"When significant initiatives critical to business strategy fail to meet their highest-priority stated goals."*

When the breakdown affects everyone in the organization, we might say the organization has failed as whole, even if only a small number of actors are to blame. When this happens with small companies (such as two of the start-ups I have consulted), the source and the impact are obvious.

A start-up of 10 people grew to nearly 20 in a month to scale up for a large IBM contract. All resources were brought into alignment to serve this contract, but after roughly 8 months, the contract was cut. A manager senior to our project lead hired a truck and carted away all our work product and computers, leaving people

---

[2] Taleb's Black Swan thesis teaches that, even if we don't believe there are black swans, they may in fact exist. Statistical improbabilities occur in reality, with consequences. Applied to decision making, critical negative events with extremely low probabilities of occurrence should not be treated as irrelevant or impossible.

literally sitting at empty desks. We learned that IBM had at least three internal projects working on the same product, and they selected the internal team that delivered first. The product was IBM's version of Microsoft's XENIX operating system; the winners had wrapped IBM binders around Microsoft books and declared it done, first.

That team accomplished their effort based on time-to-market goals, beating our small firm's high-quality product strategy. However, the poor quality of the rushed product was partly to blame for its eventual failure in the marketplace. IBM failure of foresight was real, the product bombed in the market. It was not an *organizational* failure, however. Their product development moved on to other projects. Our start-up, meanwhile, folded within the year.

Small organizations have insufficient *resilience* to survive exogenous shocks such as the abrupt ending of a client project. Resilience is the capacity to respond fluidly to unforeseen events, and the ability to recover and reorganize after impacts such as loss of revenue or a market failure. Organizational *adaptability* is a closely related notion, but adaptability refers to an organization's adaptation to *external* market or competitive forces, by revising strategy or product portfolios as market conditions change. Resilience is an internal capacity of an organization to effectively allocate resources and reorganize people as situations demand change. In large organizations resilience is strengthened by the greater redundancy of human resources (people and skills), as well as financial and process resources.

The demise of our start-up was directly caused by an external decision in a contracted business situation. Strategic foresight, scenario planning, and organizational adaptability would have made no difference in this case. The external event was entirely unforeseen, even if IBM's "secret parallel projects" strategy was well-known in the industry at the time. Foresight and adaptability are externally focused, and consider the competitive and technology landscape. The business ecosystem must be navigated by a resilient organization.

Smaller firms can plan resilience into their strategic management, but it requires foresight and a willingness to explore vulnerabilities. During the dot-com boom I consulted with a rapidly growing technology company in California (Invisible Worlds). They landed hard in late 2000, along with many other technology firms and start-ups, when their venture financers pulled their funding.

However, they were able to protect and sustain their core technology investment by establishing a multiple channel development and innovation diffusion strategy. They were able to continue development of the non-proprietary product line through engaging their participation in the open source community, and providing source and guidance for some software and feature sets. However, the start-up, the organization and its business identity, disappeared during that period's washout of the dot-com start-ups, along with firms large and small.

To what extent were internal dynamics to blame for these organizational failures? In retrospect, many of the dot-com failures had insufficient or non-existent business plans, unsustainable business models, and even less organic demand for their services. Most would have failed in a normal business climate. They floated up with the rise of investor sentiment, and crashed to reality as a class of enterprises, all of them able to save face by blaming external forces for organizational failure. A phenomenon shared in common by almost all these cases was the failure of organizational learning (or its application in predictive foresight). In nearly all these cases, leaders claimed the inability to see the problem coming. We must explore and counter this persistent, hazardous social and cognitive pattern that repeatedly occurs in organizations.

NAVIGATING THE PRODUCT ORGANIZATION

An organizational architecture refers to a structural description of essential core functions, from which organizational models and hierarchies are elaborated. An architecture is a foundation: design and reorganization starts with it, and the foundation remains after the changes are made.

Structural metaphors are useful for planning and design, and continuous planning serves the purposes of resilience and adaptation. Planning may help prevent organizational failures. Not necessarily by following the plans, which are usually over-determined and often plain wrong, but rather by the very activity of planning and the collective mental models created and shared in common while planning. Consider organizational architecture as a useful planning model, providing a consistent way of addressing the structures of a large organization related to decision, process, action, and role definition for project teams.

Although management thinkers have used the term almost literally as an approach to modeling the design of organizations, the term is metaphorical. As a working theory of the organizing functions of the firm, we find at least three significant references from the early 1990's. Nadler's *Organizational Architecture*, Mintzberg's *Structure in Fives*, and the Harvard Business Review interview with Paul Allaire "The CEO as organizational architect." Organizational architecture concepts owe Henry Mintzberg's classic *The Structuring of Organizations,* and his original models of organizational types. Mintzberg (as so often the case) receives credit for the inspiration. His simple architectural view presents five operational structures found in any enterprise, regardless of design and function. They are worth revealing briefly as a baseline for understanding the origination of the architectural notion, and the relationships of knowledge-creating functions to strategic and operational departments. Figure 1 shows the five basic parts and their relative position in a vertical hierarchy. The strategic apex organizes senior leadership functions and guides corporate strategy, management, systems (technostructure), and support staff.

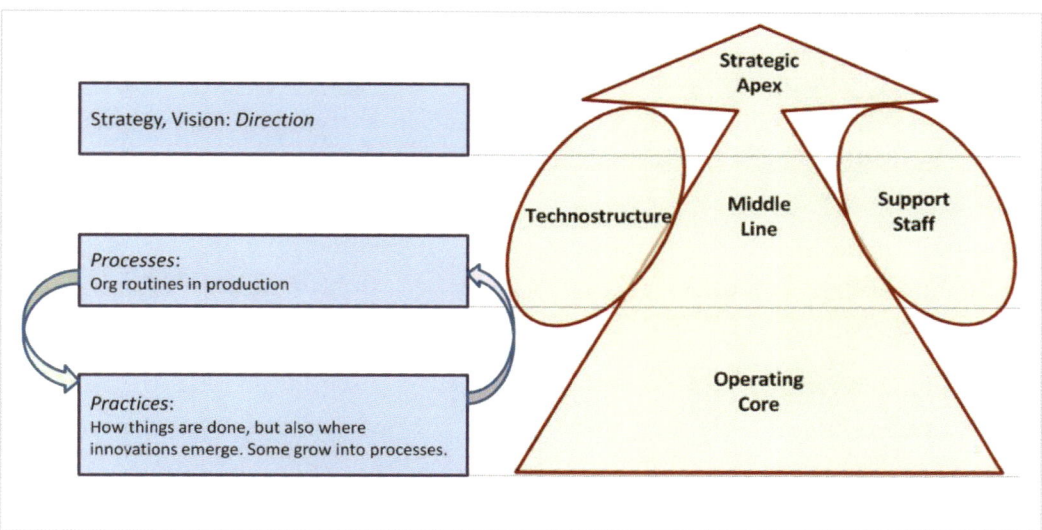

Figure 1. Mintzberg's 5 Basic Parts of an Organization.

The largest complement of the organization is contained within the operating core, as indicated by the expansive base of the figure. The middle line includes all management, excluding officers, and expanding in number and size to meet the operating core employees. Added to the Mintzberg figure are three boxes pointing to the functions at each level. We show strategy, vision and direction as central processes at the strategic apex, business processes and organizational routines managed and controlled by the middle line, and practices in the operating core. Practices are those activities performed by professional or skilled contributors that are developed and enhanced by application, repetition, and learning on projects and processes. Practices enable continuous organizational learning, since people responsible for their own contribution improve work practices over time. As some practices develop into regular patterns that generate real value, they become formalized as processes. In the early days of IT, software development started as a practice, as a craft owned totally by programmers. It was continually formalized for over 30 years or more by higher-level programming languages and the repeatable methods of business information systems methods. Software development is in some ways returning to its roots in practice with the use of popular Agile methods. User experience is another example of a practice on the verge of process institutionalization, in our case study and in many firms.

DECISIONS ACROSS ORGANIZATIONAL STRUCTURE

Organizational failures are failures of communication, at some point in their progression. The continuity of control and information exchange between macro (enterprise) and micro (information and product) architectures can be traced in the spoken and written communications within and between departments. Projects often break down in execution because information was withheld, suppressed, changed, or enhanced. Decisions are made, and original verbal events may never be recoverable.

Organizational structure and processes are major components, but the idea of "an architecture" is not merely structural. An integrated view of organizational design involves (at least) the following structures, processes, resources, and communication dynamics:

- **Structures**: Enterprise, organizational, departmental, networks.
- **Business processes**: Product fulfillment, product development, customer service.
- **Products**: Structures and processes associated with products sold to markets.
- **Practices**: User Experience, project management, software design.
- **People and roles**: Titles, positions, assigned and informal roles.
- **Finance**: Accounting and financial rules that embed priorities and values.
- **Communication rules**: Explicit and implicit rules of communication and coordination.
- **Styles of** work: Habits, how work gets done, how people work together, formal behaviors.
- **Values**: Explicit and tacit values, priorities in decision making.

All of these components are significant and necessary functions in the organizational mix, and all rely on communication to maintain roles and positions in the internal architecture. While we may find a single converging communication point (a leader) in Structures and People, these structures are largely self-organizing in practice, continuously reified through self-managing communication. They will not have a single failure point identifiable in a communication chain, because nearly all organizational conversations are redundant and will be propagated by other voices and in other formats.

Transparently bad decisions are typically caught in their early stages of communication, and are further mitigated through mediation by other players. Organizations are resilient when they have plenty of backup, such as surplus resources and multiple communications channels. However, in the process of "backup," we commonly find cover-up, the emergence of consensus denial around the biggest failures. The kinds of stories people want to hear get reinforced and repeated. Everyday failures are easier to see compared to major breakdowns.

So are we even capable of sensing the imminence of an event or signal that heralds a major failure in our organizational systems? Organizational failure is not a popular issue and we find few business books dealing with the matter. Certainly those advocating that we learn from failure are encouraging the right behaviors; if we "fail faster to succeed sooner" as IDEO's David Kelley suggests, we learn sooner than our competition what NOT to do. I might add that it's less risky for a creative design firm such as IDEO to "fail fast," because their failures involve concepts and prototypes, long before engineering specs are delivered. United Airlines might have more trouble operationalizing this notion. Computer systems firms such as Marketline, using monolithic "waterfall" development processes may have trouble adapting. Employees can handle a project failure; but to acknowledge that the firm broke down—as a system—is another matter.

Figure 2 shows a Mintzberg "organigraph" of the case organization, simplifying the essential organizational architecture (People, Process, Product, and Project) to reveal differences in structure, process, and timing among the development projects. In order to show the multiple contingencies in a typical product firm, the organigraph shows the temporal linkages of projects rather than a true hierarchical organization chart. Mintzberg (1999) suggests the very purpose of the organigraph is to "reflect the varied ways people organize themselves at work today." In this company, *time*—time to market, release schedules, resource allocation—was a constant, dominant driver of organizational behavior.

We can often locate the origination of product failures in development projects, and at times, in the upstream activity of product definition and concept formation. Often the wrong product is brought to market, defined incorrectly from the outset, but just as often the product concept "drifts" during development in attempts to adapt to a changing marketplace.

WE TRIED TO WARN YOU

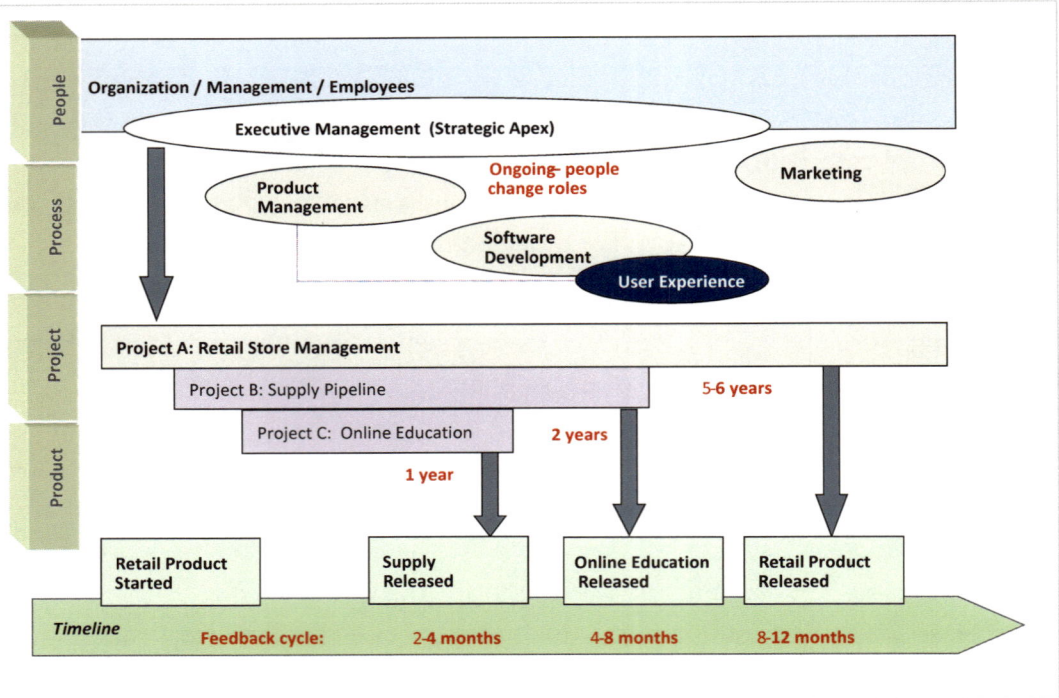

Figure 2. Organigraph of Marketline by product/project timeframe.

In Figure 2, the timeline labeled "Feedback cycle" shows how smaller projects cycled user and market feedback quickly enough to impact product decisions and design, usually before initial release. Due to the significant scale, major rollout, and long sales cycle of the Retail Store Management product, the market feedback (sales) took most of a year to reach executives. After such a duration, the original sources of user feedback and insight were nearly untraceable.

Over the project lifespan of Retail Store Management, the organization:

- Planned a "revolutionary" not evolutionary product.
- Spun off and even sequestered the development team—to "innovate" undisturbed by the pedestrian projects of the going concern.
- Spent years developing "best practices," for technology, development, and the retail practices embodied in the product.

- Kept the project a relative secret from the rest of the company, until close to initial release.
- Evolved technology significantly over time as paradigms changed, starting as an NT client-server application, then distributed database, finally a Web-enabled rich client interface.

Large-scale failures can occur when a real-world domain of work and the potential user activities are not well understood. All product managers understand the need to identify the best balance of priorities among all requirements for a new product. Product requirements are typically balanced between the customer needs and the business model and revenue requirements of the enterprise. However, even a strong customer needs focus will not afford insight into user acceptance, motivations and workplace constraints without observation and participation at the front lines. Ignoring the realities of a user's workplace, not just the marketplace, results in weak product uptake. When a new product cannot fail, organizations will prohibit acknowledging even minor failures, with cumulative failures to learn building from small mistakes. This can lead to one very big failure at the product or organizational level.

The situation shown in Figure 2 generates many opportunities for communications to fail, leading to decisions based on biased information. From an abstract perspective, modeling the inter-organizational interactions as "boxes and arrows," we may think it just a management exercise to "fix" these problems. In reality, these dynamics are nearly irreparable once set in motion.

PROJECT DYNAMICS AND FAILURE MECHANISMS

While the organizational studies literature has much to offer about organizational learning mechanisms, we find few direct links to failure dynamics from the perspectives of product management, management processes, or organizational communications.

Researching failure is similar to researching the business strategies of firms that went out of business (e.g., Raynor, 2007). They are just unavailable for us to analyze, they are either covered-up embarrassments, or they become transformed over time and much expense into "successes."

In *The Strategy Paradox*, Raynor describes the "survivor's bias" of business research, pointing out that internal data is unavailable to researchers for the dark matter of the business universe, those that go under. Raynor shows how a large but unknowable proportion of businesses fail pursuing nearly "perfect" business strategies. (This is what's meant by "go big or go home." Going concerns that avoid "going big" often survive because of their mediocre strategies, avoiding the hazards of failure risked by extreme strategies).

A major difference in the current discussion is that organizational failure as discussed here does not necessarily bring down the firm, at least not directly, as a risky strategy might do. However, product and market failures often lead to complete reorganization of divisions and large projects. These actions are not adaptive to business conditions, but merely emergency reactions to a crisis. The recovery from product failure and its reaction may set business and organizational strategy back by years, as ground is lost in the marketplace, brand share and reputation is diminished along with trust, and current products lines may be overtaken by smaller competitors who adapted to the marketplace for effectively.

One reason we are unlikely to assess the organization as having failed is the temporal difference between failure triggers and the shared experience of observable events. Any product failure will affect the organization, but some failures are truly organizational. They may be more difficult to observe.

If a prototype design fails quickly (within a single usability test period), and a project starts and fails within six months, and a product takes perhaps a year to determine its failure—what about an organization? We should expect a much longer cycle from the originating failure event to a general acknowledgement of failure, perhaps 2-5 years.

There are different timeframes to consider with organizational versus project or product failure. In the Marketline case study, the failure was not observable until after a year or so of unexpectedly weak sales, with managers and support dealing with customer resistance to the new product.

However, decisions made years earlier set the processes in place that eventuated as adoption failure. Tracing the propagation of decisions through resulting actions, we also find huge differences in the responsive time of communications between the levels of hierarchy (found in all large organizations). News and advice has immediate impact laterally, as colleagues in the same project have a common effort at stake, and the information makes a difference. Contrary or "bad news" traveling up the chain will be subject to a hierarchical game of "telephone," where each repeat of the original claim is weakened or adjusted to fit the narrowing audience of listeners. By the time an executive hears the issue mentioned, it will probably be buried in a stack of Powerpoint charts, at best, as an aside. Recall the non-urban legend of NASA engineers using dense Powerpoint slides to communicate up the chain of command, among other issues, the bad news about the possibility of damage to heat tiles weakening the resistance of the space shuttle to re-entry conditions, which enabled the destruction of the *Columbia* in its final mission in 2003.

Failures can occur when a chain of related decisions, based on bad assumptions, cascade over time into actions and feedback. These micro-failures may have occurred at the time as "mere" communication problems. As with the known problem of the space shuttle tiles, communications are overlooked or ignored even when they are attempted. These issues are written off by organizational participants as what Taleb calls "black swan" events, possibilities of devastating impact that are so rare that we can conceive of them, but ignore their likelihood. So when facing a panel of busy superiors, people from the "operating core" can fall prey to groupthink. Without rock solid evidence or personal conviction, we find it much easier to go with the corporate narrative.

In our case study, the original product requirements were defined based on industry best practices, guided by experts and key customers, but excluded end user feedback. Requirements were managed by senior product managers and were maintained as frozen specifications so that development decisions and project tasks could be managed. Requirements become treated as-if validated merely by their continuing existence without being contested and by their direct advocacy by product managers. However, with no evaluation by end users of embodied requirements—no process prototype was demonstrated—product managers and developers had no insight into dire future consequences of product architecture decisions.

Consider the timing of user research and design decisions necessary for almost any project. A cycle of less than a month is a typical loop for integrating design recommendations from usability evaluation results into an iterative product lifecycle. Within that month cycle, recommendations must be selected for priority, translated to designs models (wireframes or prototypes), and must be assessed for development. Then they must be coded, tested, integrated, retested, and reviewed. The case project was managed as a large-scale incremental development model with a full waterfall build in each increment.

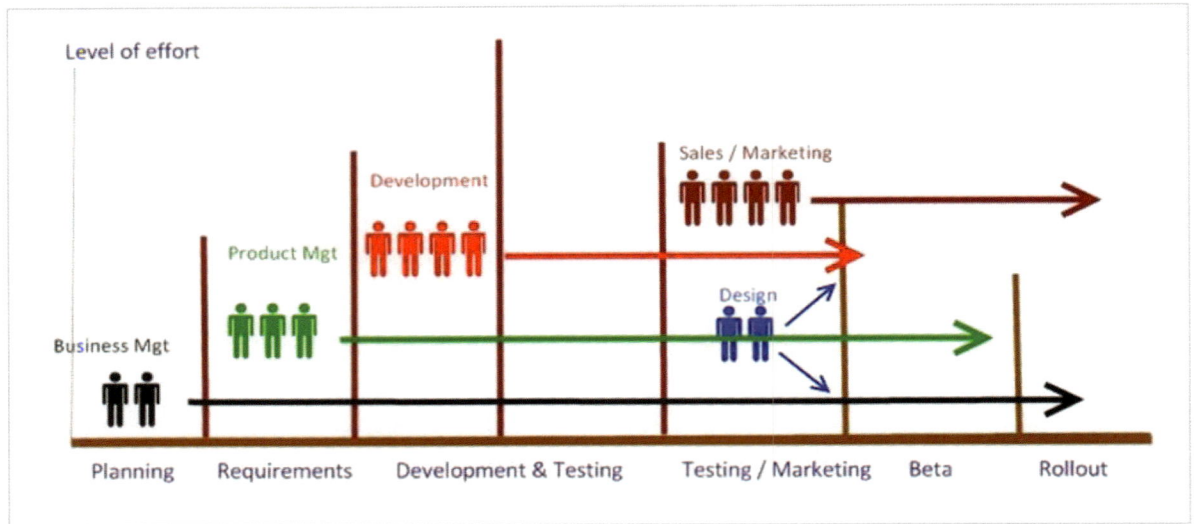

Figure 3. Late introduction of UX/Design in lifecycle negates foresight.

If the design process is NOT agile or iterative, we see the biggest temporal gaps of all. As development progresses, the costs of repair exponentially increase. Changing a requirement is the cheapest embodiment to "fix," changing a design a bit more expensive. Changing deployed code is very expensive indeed. Ironically, it may be politically less acceptable (for those who do not "own" the requirements) to argue against a requirement than to point out the problem once obvious in the design. Therefore, we hold our fire, and wait until the problem emerges in testing or in the field. We cannot travel back in time to revise requirements. The sole exception may be when a tester declares a problem a "show-stopper," but anyone with experience in the world of today's product development knows this would be an unlikely call from any internal usability evaluator. (Such assertions from an external evaluator could be ignored; evidence the consultant was uninformed about the "real" customer environment.)

In a waterfall or incremental development process, which remains typical for these large-scale products—usability tests and user feedback often have little meaningful impact on requirements and development.

Effectively organized field visits or user evaluations often reveal problems that might lead to eventual product failure in a market if overlooked. Given the political context of the typical organization, will an evaluator have the power to stand up on the terms of their data and stop the assembly line? Field visits, customer meetings, market research, and by extension, usability research are often fraught with expectations about the need for a "successful" engagement or test. We often find customer experience opportunities burdened by management intervention to the detriment of obtaining authentic and credible user data.

Usually the organization colludes—implicitly and professionally—to defend the project timelines, to save face, to maintain leadership confidence. Usability colludes to ensure they have a future on the project (or a job). So it goes with macro failures; everyone is partly to blame, but nobody accepts responsibility. The project survives, relationships survive, but the product itself might not.

PARTICIPATING IN INNOVATION

The position of lateral leadership articulated here may be appear opposed to mainstream management thinking. Yet it supports the emerging trend toward interdependent leadership in organizational development, where all members of an organization take responsibility for leadership within a cooperative network of participation and communication. And the results of this approach are quickly observable in real organizations and situations.

Such an inclusive, cross-disciplinary perspective is increasingly accepted within management practice, but is unevenly applied across firms. We believe that inclusive participatory management will lead to more competitive organizations, but many factors affect this claim in practice. The potential for change arises from the value of diffusing certain artifact-producing skills (prototyping), thinking models (strategic innovation), and valuable data representations (user field data). These "methods in motion" have the capacity to create considerable organizational disruption, as their value transcends any single discipline or intra-firm monopoly on the power of their use. The socializing approach we disclose diffuses the process innovation and ensures inclusive participation, as people discover and use the new practices through organic social networks. This lateral diffusion also constrains the usual competition for organizational power that arises when negotiating resource availability for skills or services that have become desirable.

Observations and research experience across firms show that the innovation projects (product development) supported by continual and meaningful user-led design guidance are the most successful projects in a firm's portfolio. The emerging practices of user experience design, ranging from concept ideation to brand and product design, from visual communication to usability research, have become proven innovation practices in product development. Since most UX functions are also user-facing activities, these practices are further advantaged by their access to the reality-based world of real user data. Between practices and data, user experience design is also in a unique position to facilitate organizational change.

However, the user experience function in particular often fails to leverage their opportunity for recognizing and leading change. Other knowledge-centric (R&D) or customer-facing (sales) functions also fit this "missed opportunity " pattern. Sales management rarely communicates the strategic impact of their insights from the field—they are often the most tactical group in the firm and have no incentive for rocking the boat (unless sales are weak due to a definable feature deficit compared to competitors). This tactical focus may also explain why UX staff (in my experience) rarely has direct contact with Sales, even though both have uniquely qualified access to customers in the field. Research and Development (R&D) likewise has unique access to insights about technology adoption and are able to forecast the rate of change better than other departments. However, in most firms they rarely advise Marketing or Strategy about product decisions after a go-to-market strategy has been adopted. The typical R&D horizon works from a foresight horizon of about 3-5 years, and product marketing, only 1-3 years.

User experience groups often sit between the clearly-defined stalwarts of product management and development, and must strike a balance and serve both as internal customers. This traditionally vulnerable identity inhibits leadership. When "bad news" emerges from the field (or from the lab) as foresight, its presentation is considerably softened by the academically-trained analysts and psychologists often found in UX organizations in large enterprises. (Human factors psychologists are notorious for saying "it depends" when pushed to explain ambiguous user behavior; it's no wonder that UX equivocates when user feedback might suggest a major change in strategic direction).

In the case study example, observe that none of the organizational advantages inherent in user experience design were taken up. Even with limited access to real-world user data, feedback on early prototypes, or user surveys, the feedback remained tactical. Figure 2 shows that the newly developed function of user experience (UX) was established as a small group of matrixed staff positioned under Product (Software) Development. While not the optimal location for a creative user-facing group, they were supported in this position with ready access to supportive management and resources for prototyping. However, as user feedback was gathered and continued to conflict with product strategy, its powerless location became suboptimal. Software and UX are expected to implement requirements, not to question them. In this case, the formal positioning of UX as sub to Development rendered their advice almost useless.

We could recommend (in this organization) actions such as educating project managers about UX, creating marketing-friendly usability sessions to enlist support from internal competitors, making well-timed pitches to senior management with line management support, et cetera.

In practice, it usually does not work out this way. From a macro perspective, when large projects that "cannot fail" are managed aggressively in large organizations, the user experience function is typically subordinated to project management, product management, and development. User experience—whether expressing its user-centered design or usability roles—can be perceived as introducing new variables to a set of baselined requirements, regardless of lifecycle model (waterfall, incremental, or even Agile). While a flexible orientation to requirements makes sense in the upstream definition phase, requirements are progressively locked down as a project proceeds in development. Other disciplines rarely push back on requirements, as they have little insight into rationale for asserting a business need for change. However, fixes and innovative features are often generated directly from UX field engagements. Given the late-breaking news quality of customer field research, latitude should be planned into scheduling and resource availability to ensure these opportunities are captured.

THE POWER OF CUSTOMER EVIDENCE

User experience practice often promotes an authoritative position toward influencing changes to product requirements conferred by their privileged access to user data. In uncertainty situations, attempts to leverage this position can makes matters worse, as it tends to polarize team members into opposing camps. Under the organizational pressures of executing a top-down managed product strategy, project leaders often close ranks around the objectives. The expectation of total alignment to strategy is made clear to all team members. Late-arriving user experience "findings" that could conflict with internal strategy will be treated as threatening, not helpful.

With such large, cross-departmental projects, signs of warning that are drawn from user data can simply be disregarded, as not fitting the current organizational frame. In addition, if user studies are performed and reported, significant conflicts with strategy can be discounted as the analyst's interpretation. Internal UX team members may also be too committed to project outcomes to assign dire consequences to their observations. It also exposes their culpability for the impossible expectation of not having designed a perfect product in advance of the evaluation. At least when UX/user research is conducted by external consultants, they share no blame in the design and may have experience in detecting leading issues and presenting the "bad news" tactfully to the product team.

Market research usually does not expose these types of conflicts for the primary reason that it is commissioned by the department (Marketing) that has the most to gain from executing a successful product strategy. Market research is primarily concerned with maximizing opportunities for growth of current products from current, meaning past-based, consumer behaviors. Product adoption, a foresight problem, is very difficult to assess with focus groups and surveys.

Market research is notoriously insensitive to the emergent responses of end users. It is responsive to determining aggregate market demand for types of products, classes of features, and for comparing sets of alternatives included in product offerings. Market research should also be seen as detecting at best only current behaviors, more typically trailing indicators, not leading behaviors. Survey and focus group respondents are unable to indicate or imagine true future scenarios in the context of questions about current practice or well-known features. Aggregate measures cannot identify the specific problems that occur only in user interaction and tacit knowledge revealed in the surprises and reactions disclosed in the context of a real work setting.

User research (UX research) teases out the reasons why a feature is unused or an interface is found difficult to use. Usability and user field studies can also forecast trouble ahead better than most other instruments. (By the time market research indicates trouble, it can be too late to respond effectively, especially for first-movers). By mapping business and product requirements to the field evaluation scenarios, teams can gain insight into the customer priorities and compare them to the business goals and requirements. Measuring these differences can expose gaps in strategy and customer need that lead to feature or adoption failure.

There are battles an emerging practice cannot win. New organizational routines require time to be structured and diffuse. The values of cross-disciplinary participation seem obvious, but take time to take hold in a longstanding culture. Managers (and UX professionals) must draw on inner resources of experience, intuition, and common sense and develop alternatives to standard methods and processes. As anthropologist Bruno Latour (2008) recently noted, we are dealing with "matters of concern" rather than "matters of fact," and must allow for some retrenchment into existing routines while new practices are socialized. Therefore, the quality of interpersonal communications may make more of a difference, initially, than the customer data. By acknowledging that such interpretations may be unpopular, the new advocacy role presents itself as a fair and unbiased agent mediating the user's perspective to managers and stakeholders. We should recognize that this mediation occurs within an organization that is comprised, realistically speaking, of a collection of engaged members who must constantly revise their own mental models of the multiple forces converging on the same large project. These mental models are also significantly driven by organizational defenses, which serve the purpose of keeping members focused on tasks at hand and ignoring threatening issues or conflicting evidence.

According to Harvard's Chris Argyris (1992), organizational defensive routines are "any routine policies or actions that are intended to circumvent the experience of embarrassment or threat by bypassing the situations that may trigger these responses. Organizational defensive routines make it unlikely that the organization will address the factors that caused the embarrassment or threat in the first place."

Due to organizational defenses most managers will place the blame for product or market failures on individuals rather than the consequences of poor decisions or other root causes, and will deflect critique of the general management or decision making processes. Argyris identifies double-loop learning as a progressively adapted response to such defenses. When managers are willing to look at underlying causes for failures (or errors), they find that real advantage can be applied by attempting to change organizational belief systems.

"Double-loop" learning occurs when an error is detected and corrected in ways that involve the modification of an organization's underlying norms, policies and objectives.

Significant research work has followed their theoretical platform by exploring how people accomplish the project of building a more reflective organizational culture. Changing norms involves changing tacit and deeply held values that persist in organizations longer than most employees do. In other articles (Jones, 2002), I describe how organizational values are created, persist, and change over long periods of time. The values that create team loyalty, organizational purpose, and a shared sense of identity also implicitly limit types of work practices, investments, and even customers. Once they've become an ultimate source of decisions, people cannot easily see the constraints they create, let alone question their impact. Organizational values are powerful precisely because people act on them every day *without* reflection.

INFLUENCING AND LEARNING OPPORTUNITIES

User experience has the privilege of being available on the front lines of product design, research, and testing. However, it does not typically carry substantial organizational authority. In a direct showdown between product management and UX, product wins every time. Product is responsible for revenue, and must live or die by the calls they make.

User experience design has the opportunity to respond their direct internal client's needs. With product management as internal client, UX can fit research and recommendations to the context of product requirements, adapting to the goals and language of requirements management. User experience, or R&D, must design sufficient variety into prototypes to be able to effectively test expected variances in preference and work practice differences. Adding variety to design concepts allows the designer to share ideas without the appearance of conflicting with set requirements. Interface and visual design alternatives can explicitly set up different scenarios that still meet the letter of the requirements. If product requirements leave insufficient opportunity for such micro-innovation, they have been written incorrectly and should be abstracted more to articulate functions and not design details.

UX research methods,, such as usability evaluation and ethnographic studies, must be constructed with clear objectives, including fit to the user's real work, the total product experience, and a focus on strategic priorities, not just favorite features. Given a set of research findings, any team member should be able to make direct determinations from the as to whether the product requirements fit the user's work and needs. The UX role is ultimately responsible for the evaluation and interpretation of user data, and the organizational communication regarding its meaning. The test objectives, as user responses to interaction, should be clearly observable in video recordings and the test data.

Because the user experience role is closest to the end user throughout the entire product development lifecycle, they play a vital early warning role for product requirements and adoption issues. However, since that is often not an explicit role, it must be supported through credibility, influence and well-timed communications.

In a growing organization, user experience practice will become explicitly organized and will grow with management support. The practice, skills, and methods are well defined in the growing practitioner literature. In the literature, we find authors often make assessments from their own experience to recommend best practices for user experience management or organizational change. Since these are written from a UX disciplinary point of view, these suggestions often overlook several major conflations: The variety of conditions that occur in large vs. small organizations, workplace/IT systems vs. websites and online products, and project management vs. practice management. A large organization functions as a complex system, and simple recommendations from a single discipline are insufficient to satisfy the variety of ongoing and connected issues in the system.

INTEGRATING THE MULTIDISCIPLINARY ORGANIZATION

The organizational scenarios in this discussion should not be considered advocacy to establish the user experience role as a new force for organizational change. Such a position misses the point; every role and function should be an advocate for strategy and execution, organizational learning and change. UX's position, located between customers and the organization, offers us insight into organizational dynamics that other roles do not afford. Since an important role of user experience is to mediate between product users and product makers, we might learn from the organizational learning or ignoring of user data and the interpretations generated by this role.

In many firms, UX has little independence and little or no authority to influence requirements definition. In the case study, a small UX group served as a dotted-line report fewer than three competing authorities. That being the case, by the time formal usability tests were scheduled, requirements and development were too deeply committed to consider any significant changes from user research. With the pressures of release schedules looming, usability was both rushed and controlled. The "rush"" to test (another temporal response in failure loops) ensured user feedback was restricted to issues contained within the scope of possible change and with minor schedule impact.

As Figure 2 showed, user experience staff reported to Development management, and was further subjected to product and project management directives (following Development).

By the time usability testing was conducted, the scope was too narrowly defined to admit any valid discoveries of unplanned user responses. When user testing is not integrated into the early product definition, it may be pushed to the end of design and development, where little schedule remains to address emergent problems or even powerful innovations learned from user interaction. When test questions are framed so that only requirements are validated and unexpected findings are blocked, the test sessions become wasted opportunities. Usability test cases were defined by product managers to test user response to individual transactions, and not the systematic processes inherent in the everyday complexity of retail, service, or financial work.

- Testing occurred in a rented facility, and not in the retail store itself.
- The context of use was defined within a job role, and not in terms of productivity or throughput.
- Individual transactions (screen views) were tested in isolation, not in the context of their relationship to the demands of real work pressures—response time, database access time, ability to learn navigation and to quickly navigate between common transactions.
- Sequences of common, everyday interactions were not evaluated.

The product team's enthusiasm for the new and innovative may prevent listening to the users' authentic preferences. When taking a conventional approach, product-centric and not activity-centered view of usability, such fundamental disconnects with the user domain may not even be observable.

Many well-tested products have been released only to fail in the marketplace due to widespread user preference to maintain their current, established, well-known system. This especially so if the work practice requires considerable learning and use of an earlier product over time, as happened in our retail system case. Very expensive and well-documented failures abound due to strong user preferences and embedded practices in a long-established installed base, with notorious examples in air traffic control, government and security, hospital information systems, and transportation systems. In these mission-critical or high-risk environments, reliability of ongoing procedure is a much higher value than usability of an untested new system. High-risk or stabilized environments present significant challenges to the human factors (or user experience), as the drivers for innovation are much less important than the need for appropriate and controlled process change. The case firm perhaps failed to realize the extent to which their current flagship product was deeply embedded into retail store systems and practices. In this company, the only established customer communication channel was that of a Customer Advisory Board, a popular approach used to maintain good relationships with key customers. However, Customer Advisory Boards are essentially a venue for executives to listen to their customer's executives. There were no processes in place to update the firm's understanding of the real world of users in their work environment. Customers should not be expected to generate such feedback on their own. Gathering and rigorously interpreting user responses to business and product inquiries was traditionally a market research function, but has become a primary role of user experience, given their facility with tools and techniques for clarifying opportunities for innovation and product enhancement.

However, success is not guaranteed even so. When the UX role is itself "embedded" as part of a large team, accountable to product or project management, a natural bias emerges to expect the joint team's design to succeed. When interface designers in the UX team must also plan and conduct usability tests (as in our case study), we cannot expect a "tester" to set aside their attachment to the ownership of the product from their "designer" role. We may find the same person working in both of these two opposing roles. User experience design consultants are also constantly faced with this dilemma, but they ultimately pass on design responsibility to the client, and are also given more latitude to defend their findings to clients. With a user experience team reporting to Development, and restricted latitude for design change (due to impossible delivery deadlines), we can observe how design failures occur in spite of good work and good intentions.

We have no analytical or quantitative tools for predicting the degree of market adoption based on even well-designed usability evaluations. Determining the likelihood of product adoption failure across nationwide or international markets is a matter of judgment based on experience and insight, even with survey data of sufficient power to estimate the population. Because of the show-stopping impact of advancing such a judgment, it's unlikely the lower-status user experience role will push the case, even if it is clearly warranted from user research.

The purpose of this book is not to recommend organizational fixes based on better user experience design methods, usability evaluation, or UX management. User experience is just one of many knowledge-creating functions in product firms that serve a foresight role, that might observe the seeds of future failure in patterns of customer behavior. The chief difference is that user experience members are charged with learning about users and interpreting their behavior and preferences on behalf of the organization. Other practices with direct access to customers contribute to organizational sensemaking and decisionmaking, including market research and sales conversations. However, these other channels are not dedicated to understanding and validating innovations; that role falls to user experience.

Other members (R&D, even Marketing) may rarely witness the front lines of user interaction with new product concepts. We can cure this isolation from the user's reality by creating opportunities for observation, sitting in on field trials, attending usability sessions, joining requirements interviews. Organizations must take advantage of as many opportunities to establish "listening loops" as practical, to circulate feedback from real users throughout the organization.

LATERAL LEADERSHIP ACROSS BOUNDARIES

The socialization approach to process evolution and management prescribes an inclusive organizational leadership style. Socialization employs a distributed, lateral approach to inviting participation and cooperation from core members to peripheral members in a network. The network effect of lateral (cross-functional) organizational communications creates new channels for cooperation across departmental boundaries and coordinates organizational members when new practices and capabilities are being created and developed. These practices are most commonly formed, redesigned, and re-formed in boundary-spanning business functions that go by different names in large firms, such as Research and Development, product design, user experience, innovation management, market research, or knowledge management groups. These functions all translate knowledge from original sources to the nerve centers of the business, and have unique skill sets with much to offer to all projects in a contemporary products or services firm.

We develop the case study based on the user experience example due to its unique access to customer insights as well as its boundary-spanning character. An *established* user experience department offers significant competitive advantage to firms that can effectively meld several unique core functions: User understanding and advocacy, product design process and design craft, product execution, and user evaluation. Effective UX groups also serve project and organizational communicative functions, such as balancing product priorities, scanning technologies and potential competitors, and project and team communications. Few firms take full advantage of their user experience capabilities, and they miss out on the benefits of user-responsive management of projects and products. In most organizations user experience departments are managed like internal support groups, an efficiency service that accelerates product design, assigned to project teams to ensure usability goals are met. What if your organization encouraged *leadership* from designers and user research coordinators? How would that change team dynamics, product requirements, and project decisions?

User experience can also be seen as a short-term R&D unit assigned to product development, providing early concepts, field testing, and fitting innovations to the user need. Perhaps due to its traditionally malleable, adaptive stance UX managers often seek institutionalization of processes, to better benefit all product teams with standard practices and to improve service delivery across the organization.

User experience, as with any knowledge practice, contributes most effectively when stabilized in the organization, when it becomes a dedicated and dependable resource responsive to capacity demands. To accomplish this, managers often attempt to "institutionalize" the new practice as a route to defining (and owning) a stable organizational process. However, from a knowledge-enabling perspective, a new or emerging business function should not start with an institutionalization project, to establish its presence on the organization chart. Rather, we advocate create growing organic demand for its real value and letting it expand *laterally*.

The practices employed in a *socialization* approach flow in nearly the opposite temporal order to that of institutionalization. They represent an opposing view and process to that of "importing" industry best practices into an intact organization. Socialization requires that we create demand from internal customers, and quickly adapt the right set of priorities for skill sets to be developed in accord with the current needs of the firm.

ORGANIC GROWTH - BY DRIFT AND BY DESIGN

Returning to our case, we can examine how Marketline developed its capacity for product design and user experience in response to a rapidly emergent need. The organizational need was for a working prototype in 6 weeks for a product representing a definitive plan to recover from the acknowledged product failure. The capstone prototype was intended for a board-level presentation, setting high stakes for a significant consensus direction.

Senior management reviewed consultants for the project and my design research firm was hired to lead the effort. The new user experience team, as shown in Figure 4, started with a product manager and a project team drawn together from the few resources available with compatible backgrounds (psychology, software prototyping). While bringing competence and passionate dedication to the table, the local team also exhibited minimal traditional UX skills, and had no supporting internal resources. Management was diffused across multiple levels and departments and was in a constant state of adaptation to changing priorities. The UX project team was granted significant management autonomy, and followed a clearly-defined plan from the proposal. We treated the organization as a large network of resources, all of which *potentially* available to our ad hoc team. To learn about real customer needs, drivers, and their changing workplace in the field, we started with contextual interviews with Customer Support, to gain the internal perspective.

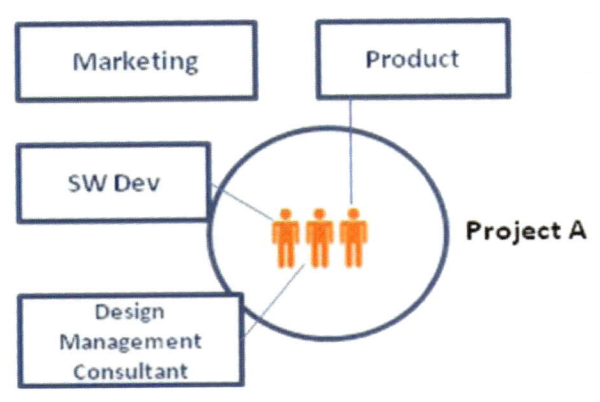

Figure 4. Initial team formed for project.

Peripheral and part-time participants from Marketing, Customer Support, and Engineering were recruited as required (Fig. 5), gaining significant grassroots support for the project and assuaging fears (rumors) that the new project might somehow bypass the company's "old hands," a common perception with new technology-driven projects.

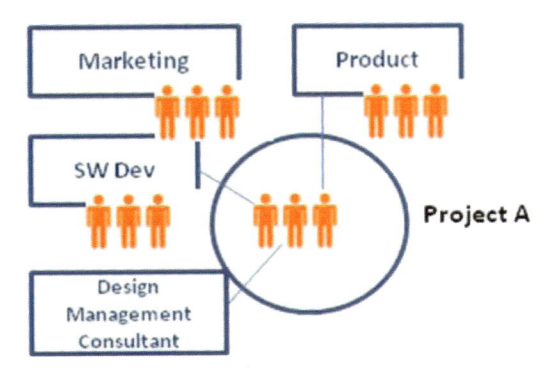

Figure 5. Project team connects across departments.

Marketing and Customer Support can often be counted on for valuable insight and sincere cooperation. Their interaction enabled us to validate and refine the inquiry instruments, which were immediately deployed to conduct a full complement of contextual interviews with field users across a range of retail stores in differing geographic regions. Details from both internal and customer sessions were employed to construct work activity models (supported by *personas*, as general user profiles, for circulation in the larger organizations). In-context user interviews and workplace observations supported the design, development and testing of three prototype variations to test a clearly-defined set of task models.

As significant business goals were met (including a successful demonstration to the board of the capstone prototype), other projects expressed interested in adopting UX practices, increasing internal demand. The positive response to the successful prototype pushed the team to the next major goal, that of redesigning the company's flagship product based on the prototype. The socialization process was birthed from this demand; the user experience team developed an appropriate low-resource impact response to the organizational need, and designed and led an internally-networked design process within a two month period.

In-house members attached to the user experience team reported to different departments (Product marketing and Software development) throughout the entire project. The design management consultant served a leadership role best characterized as *project integration*. As an external consultant, I had no decision making or resource authority, but was able to manage more effectively at this network level than a hierarchical manager could have. Communications and negotiations for resources were made as peer-to-peer requests, bypassing official channels and the usual competition for resources that occurs when sharing rare and in-demand skills.

The user experience team was expected to "evangelize" or advocate the practice and apply its ideas and methods to other projects, partly for skill practice as well as for sharing new knowledge with teams with real needs for user research or prototyping. Managers negotiated for their availability to a project by requesting UX staffing for targeted, specific tasks best suited for short-term engagements. An acting management team planned to formalize the user experience group with a dedicated organizational home and supervising manager, and new hires (interns and 1-2 full time) were planned based on demand for skills in prototyping and information architecture. While both Marketing and Engineering haggled for ownership of the nascent group, the still ad hoc UX team continued to advise and consult with other projects on the application of user-centered design and research to their products (Fig. 6). These lateral communications diffused through the organizational networks and sparked interest widely across projects and departments.

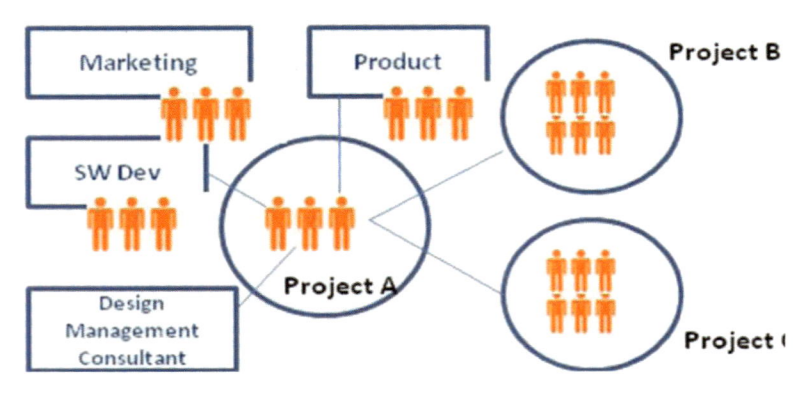

Figure 6. UX team project shared skills to accelerate projects.

Product managers leading other projects were especially interested in two UX tasks for their products, prototyping and user research. These skills were not available through other resource channels in the firm (except by contracting with external firms, which was done occasionally, with widely varying results). By this time the user experience group had achieved wide visibility and significant management interest, and managers were planning for the hires to support the additional resources needed.

However, a new routine had become established by the socialization approach. A participatory approach had taken hold in a traditional hierarchical organizational. A conservative top-down company culture had enabled and encouraged an emerging leadership style that held the possibility of learning from mistakes, learning from users in the field, and sharing resources for the good of the entire organization.

ORGANIZATIONAL PROCESS SOCIALIZATION

We attempted to recover the firm's leadership position in the marketplace by rapidly designing and showing a hybrid product to key customers to demonstrate that the company was back on track with an innovative upgrade to the flagship product. The team created an updated Windows-based user interface "wrapper" that would serve the purpose of a transition interface for both new users and experienced customers. The new user interface incurred no impact on the fundamental architecture or data model, and was quickly implemented and field tested.

The firm enjoyed the fortunate market position of brand leadership, strong market share, and flagship product loyalty. The flagship product had continued to enjoy a healthy reputation, even if sales had flattened, and the current product line customers had not seen a compelling rationale to switch to the new product upon its rollout. A large current customer base had embedded the routines of the current (aging technology) flagship product deeply into their work practices. They refused to migrate to the new "best-practices" based product noted in the case, so action was required to enhance the user interface for new (younger) users who faced a steep learning curve with the old user interface (UI).

Rather than establish a new department, and hire new or pull staff from other functions, we leveraged existing, experienced people (using "internal contracts") to obtain commitments for staff hours and deliverables for the project associated with the user interface wrapper.

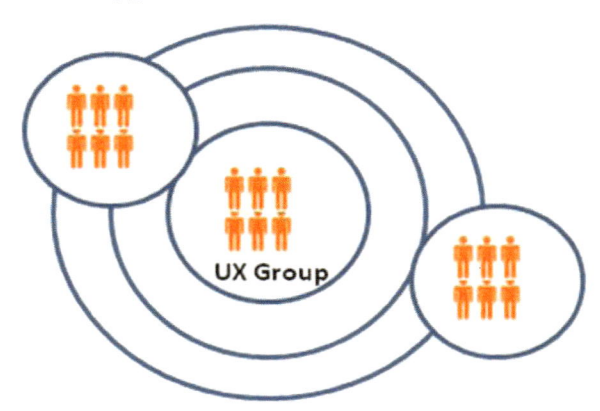

Figure 7. Project team connects across departments.

With the term *socialization* we describe a peer-to-peer diffusion to integrate emerging processes and new (user experience) skills into a changing organizational structure. This should be clarified with respect to Nonaka's (1994) description of socialization as a phase in the knowledge creation cycle (Fig. 8). Nonaka refers to socialization as the way in which employee tacit knowledge (know how) is learned from others in the social practices of everyday work activity. People working in knowledge practices of any sort (UX, R&D, Marketing) develop repertoires of knowledge and skill from tacit-tacit knowledge exchange, rightly understood as a social process of learning and evolutionary skill enhancement. In our case we are elevating the focus from individual knowledge and corporate knowledge creation to knowledge practice creation. Socialization is expressed as a many-to-many interpersonal exchange of new knowledge and skill within a department and across the organization. It is clearly analogous to Nonaka's knowledge socialization, which continues in the knowledge creating cycle with externalization, where tacit knowledge is expressed explicitly for the purposes of formal knowledge sharing.

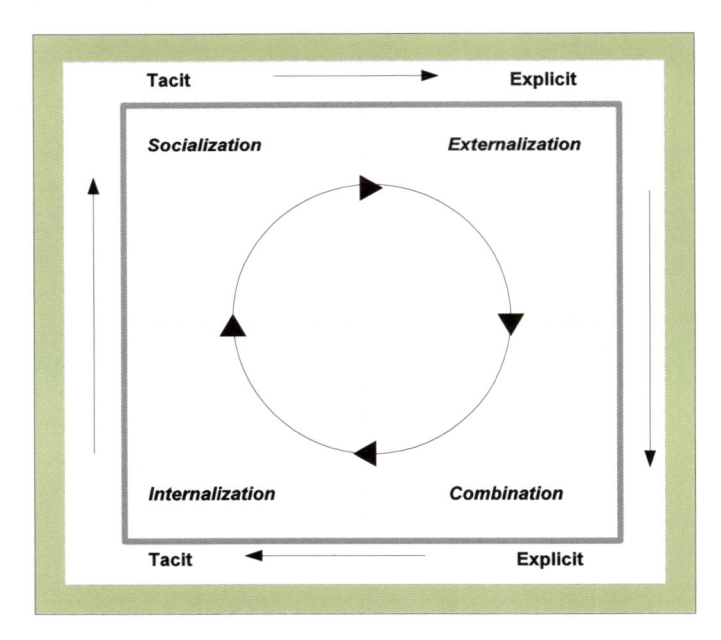

Figure 8. Socialization in Nonaka's knowledge creation cycle.

In *process* socialization, we can view the formalization of a new knowledge process as an externalization in the organization, expressed in the development of artifacts such as prototypes, and distribution of knowledge products such as user research reports and presentations. The socialized process cycle continues with combination, wherein the organization's existing structures and management explicitly engage the services of the developing practice area, and combine its new skill set with current skills and practices, adapted to the context of projects.

Process socialization was not developed with Nonaka's theory in mind. As a foundation theory of knowledge creation, Nonaka has been proven effective as a validation of observed behaviors, after the fact, not necessarily as guidance for design. Process socialization, an emergent organizational innovation, developed from a pressing need for action by energizing a small number of team members and available resources. A more elaborated process would have required more planning, longer duration, and might have achieved very different results. As the project unfolded, we recognized how socialization provided a faster, more productive alternative to top-down institutionalization. Formal management processes require an organization to establish a home base for the new function or department, with defined job roles, appropriate skills, a training plan, and management added to the hierarchy to coordinate the new practices.

Forced institutionalization can result in "brittle" organizational structures, lacking the resilience that accrues to processes cultivated from real internal demand and cross-disciplinary dialogue. Premature formalizing of process draws resources away from established management teams within a department or division, by recruiting top performing employees who are naturally interested in the new challenges presented by initiating a developing practice. Abruptly establishing a new user experience department would have violated cultural norms in this traditionally organized firm, creating the impression of a new internally competing group. The "new kid on the block" impact would have been more likely to attract responses of resentment rather than the cooperation we found in the peer-to-peer, low-key socialization approach.

The organizational/UX consultant played a significant role in socializing new practices. Organizations often allow an outside expert retained on a project to provide unique, unforeseen consulting services for an emerging and temporary engagement. Having a consultant perform and model the roles and skills that will be required for a new department minimizes the sense of any threat to established departments competing for resources. A consultant can exercise their autonomy, and can serve as a proxy manager in the early stages of socialization, experimenting with new practices and asking favors that employees and managers would not consider. People in lateral roles to UX then learn the practices through their participation in the UX-centric project. In successive iterations of prototyping, we included software engineers, customer support staff, product managers, and executives in design, pilot testing, and internal reviews. Through what Jean Lave (1991) calls "legitimate peripheral participation," people were asked to materially interact with the project and gradually increase their understanding of the contributions of UX practices and its internal products.

We believe and have observed that socialization enables a longer-term, better understood, and incremental adoption of organizational processes that occurs when people adopt practices in action, in response to a genuine need for skill and process development.

ORGANIZATIONS AS SELF-PROTECTION SYSTEMS

Notwithstanding the dramatic and interconnected institutional failures in 2008 in the global financial industry, organizations of people are "designed" to survive. They will fail at times when pursuing extreme business strategies in a competitive marketplace, or as in the unique situation of 2008, following an inherently risky strategy adopted by an entire industry. In either case, the internal communication dynamics remain very similar. An extreme focus on the projects based on market-facing competitive strategy can limit sensitivity to communications that inform organizational members of their internal health and resource strength. Recall that the Chief Risk Officer of Freddie Mac had explicitly warned the CEO 4 years before their collapse. In an organizational culture where a CEO will ignore their Risk Officer's warnings, mid-level and higher managers may be openly hostile to the contrarian signals from customer impressions that threaten the current strategy. Organizations behave in this way as collective self-protection systems, enabling and preserving a preferred trajectory of collective action, a "strategy," but incurring risks from inattention to alternative courses of action sufficiently adaptive in a changing market reality.

Most large organizations that endure become internally resilient as an organizational response to changing conditions. While a flexible strategic posture is characteristic of adaptability to external events, resilience is an internal or "inbound" collective attitude or even skill. Adaptive organizations construct sensing processes, which we call early warning systems that inform decision makers about the status of situations, progress of action, or emergent threats and competition. These processes might be better conceived as innovation sensing systems. An innovation sensing capacity informs the decisions for current innovation projects (short-range strategy) and for future options (long range strategy) that might be selected as business conditions emerge into view. Innovation sensing directly informs senior management decision making for project portfolio management, stage-gate decisions, product marketing, strategic communications and brand support, organizational development, and even training needs. These processes help the firm manage risk as conditions change, and build competitive resources in response to significant challenges.

Organizations develop resilience over time. The risk of individual or project failure is distributed across an ever-larger number of employees, reducing risk through assumed due diligence in execution. The distributed social networks of people working in large companies often prevent the worst decisions from gaining traction. The same networks also sustain poor decisions when they are major decisions, supported by management, and creatures of the company culture. These directions and choices cannot be directly challenged by contrarian data. Groupthink also prevails when people agree to maintain silence about bad decisions. No individual wants to be the first to risk breaking the code of conformity around an undiscussable issue, or one in which we have no authority or power to change. We convince ourselves that leadership will win out over the risks; the strategy will work if we give it time.

Argyris' organizational learning theory reveals how people in large organizations are often unable to acknowledge the long-term implications of learning situations. People are generally proficient at learning from their own everyday mistakes. Employees are not typically aware enough of "what the organization knows" to take responsibility for the implications of information. In our case study, employees were often unable to formulate a meaningful pattern from the weak signal of a user complaint back to the larger failure in progress that the organization was accommodating.

In Argyris' double-loop learning, the goal is learn from an outcome and reconfigure the governing variables of the situation's pattern to avoid the problem in the future. (Single-loop learning is merely changing one's actions in response to the outcome). However, double-loop learning requires people to attend to and understand the governing variables, an analytical task which itself must be learned. Argyris' research suggests all organizations have difficulties in double-loop learning. People build defenses against this learning because it requires difficult work: confrontation, reflection, and change of governance, decision processes, and values-in-use. It's much easier to just change one's own behavior.

More recently, Carol Dweck, author of *Mindset: The New Psychology of Success,* shows how an open attitude toward continual learning from experience corresponds to growth and success more reliably than talent or schooling. She calls this a growth mindset. Applied to organizations, firms that reinforce attitudes of perfectionism, leadership by personality (designated star performers), and "not failing" may paradoxically sow the seeds of larger failure. So-called individual contributors are less likely to develop or express their own leadership, in everyday work or emerging situations, when the organization has anointed certain styles of leading or communicating as a preferred direction. Finally, when members are discouraged or disallowed to fail in small ways, while trying their skills or learning to lead, they will avoid risking their reputations on larger achievement or worthy aspirations. The culture reinforces the admonition to avoid looking bad at all costs. This avoidance behavior (which is typically just everyday "looking good" social behavior) leads to people avoiding responsibility for small problems, which may build into larger, shared problems that lead to failure. However, when an entire product or organization fails, no single person can be blamed. We all fail together, just as we all win together.

INNOVATION SENSING AND ORGANIZATIONAL LEARNING

User experience, R&D, market research, sales, and any other function that attends closely to real customers can play a significant role as early innovation sensing and early warning for market adoption failure. In our particular case study, we found critical user feedback and its appropriate interpretation played a key role in alerting the firm to possible problems with the product strategy. As we found, context-sensitive customer research provides a powerful channel for discovering insights (or bad news) about potential user adoption issues. The same channel offers, perhaps, the best means of identifying meaningful solutions to the product or interaction issues discovered. Focus groups, survey research, web analytics, and usability research are all useful in their applications, but they do not gain access to contextual understanding of the real activities and available scope of choices of customer and users. They give no insight into user *sensemaking*, so these research modes cannot help us understand why a customer decided *not* to adopt a new product. We lack insight into their meaningful contexts, competing activities, and possibilities for action.

The case study shows that the organization had access to compelling facts and rationale for making serious course corrections to a current product strategy, but they chose not to act upon the information. So, how would we characterize the underlying root causes? Do the organizational dysfunctions originate from communication, corporate culture, conflicts of personal and corporate values, or tensions with power differences in the hierarchy? Can we even separate these factors, if we are truly facing the complexity of wicked problems in organizational design? Considering just some of the organizational communication issues, barriers to communicating an informed judgment include:

- **Organizational defenses.** Defensive habits prevent people from advancing their experiences and theories before noticeable failures occur.

- **Marginalized participation.** In large organizations, field-level and user feedback emerges from lower-status positions, and people in these roles may find political barriers to communicating the full impact of research. Staff contributors are burdened by the inherent demand to make their boss look good in the organization, so they may finesse bad news.

- **Organizational compartmentalization.** The reporting structure colors the message. People in Development, Sales, or User Experience will have difficulty advancing cases with strategic implications. User research indicating threats to product adoption may be dismissed, as adoption is treated as a Marketing issue.

- **Groupthink and peer protection.** People on teams protect each other, and non-professional (part-time or new) user researchers may acquiese to a team's case that the user feedback was erroneous or insufficient to make conclusions.

- **Timing**. By the time such judgments may be formed, the timeframes for realistic responsive action have disappeared, leading to withholding the communication.

Organizational learning cuts both ways. While a learning culture may (realistically) require years to evolve, the effective communicator must also *learn the organization*, responding to the different styles and venues for communication. Unfortunately, learning the organization takes the form of a tacit, internalized process of accommodation. Newer employees and consultants often proffer feedback directly without regard to organizational positions in the matter, since these relationships will not yet have been internalized as learning.

If taking a stand on the implications of serious customer evidence, small group or one-on-one meetings may be employed to test the feedback and progressively build a case. Organizational leaders may have gathered similar responses from alternative channels and are reluctant to interfere with well-executed projects, even if operating on some false assumptions. A private sharing of significant findings and well-grounded opinions allows the executive to make their own connections and use the new evidence as independent, confirmatory data. On the other hand, they may have compelling alternative stories, or "rival hypotheses" for the behaviors observed, based on other market data unavailable to the customer-facing or product teams.

Consider the different alternatives available for presenting any such case for general organizational sensemaking. User data interpreted as bad news for a new product innovation will typically be resisted. The invested owners and stakeholders in the project's success will have reasonable explanations and a defense for the established plan. If the interpretations from customer research can be validated and clarified, the responsible organizational actor must plan a communications strategy to present data and conclusions. A definitive personal choice may be necessary in such cases, between the future prospects of a strategy or one's own job and career status. Given the stakes in the situation, business or research consultants involved with organizational projects might expect to be recruited to prepare and present the case. The ethics of deflecting organizational responsibility are a matter for deeper discussion; nevertheless, in a typically dysfunctional communication environment, third-party intervention can be considered a legitimate strategy.

ADAPTIVE ORGANIZATIONAL DESIGN

Socialization is situated as an alternative to formal institutionalization and management of knowledge-creating practices, for the purposes of establishing or enhancing a new competency. While neither a methodology or a management theory, this orientation toward organizational design is based on systems thinking, organizational learning theory, and participatory co-creation. Socialization enables rapid creation of new business functions or processes requiring specific and hard-to-find skills that normally require significant learning, development time, and employee investment. It allows organizations to leverage their current capacities by foraging available skills and related practices in the organization under the call of an emergent leadership opportunity.

I admit uncertainty regarding the effectiveness of socialization in redesigning or enhancing *traditional* functions such as customer service or marketing. While these may be flexibly redesigned by a socialization process, most organizations will simply implant these core functions and support them with experienced management. Managers may tend to hazard a novel approach only when necessary, as in the case of introducing new knowledge practices. In the cases of support functions, the value of an adaptive organizational design approach may not seem apparent or necessary.

A strategic argument for socialization can be based on observations that homegrown solutions to novel organizational needs inspire the formation of unique, inimitable processes and artifacts in a company. These shared (co-created) experiences create new knowledge and resulting value that resist appropriation by competitors or transfer by employees. Local organizational solutions enable real learning, and are likely to achieve real adoption rather than the reluctant trial of external practices. Finally, locally-enacted knowledge processes become resilient, less brittle than imported best practices. When challenged by emerging situations or micro-failures, socialized practices are able to develop creative responses, and can tap into broad social networks, encouraging healthy adaptation rather than calling the vendor or consultant for support.

When externally developed processes are "imported" into established organizations, they are often likely to fail. Leaders attempting to create "change" for the sake of change may be seduced by popular management fads (such as Jim

Collins' well-known "hedgehog"), business process reengineering, formal requirements engineering (e.g. RUP), even Agile development. At Marketline, new senior managers recruited from high-visibility positions in other industries usually, sometimes religiously, imported favored management practices into the existing organization. These well-publicized management fads enable incoming executives to advance a campaign for change when the organization seemingly lacks purpose. However, in many cases and some firms, these imported fads become recognizable rituals associated with reorganizations or the attempts by new executives to make a mark upon their arrival. However, such bolt-on processes may not fit the deeper organizational culture, adapt to its routines, or fit the ongoing work ecology. Any existing organizational culture consists of years of experience with other managers, personal histories, changes in technology and practice, embedded values, tacit (socialized) knowledge about how things are done, and successes and failures, big and small. Incoming managers are subject to these pre-conditions, embedded in an organizational culture that has typically outlasted many other managers.

Yet, functionally similar management practices can be organically co-created by teams and then accelerated within the context of a significant project. Projects serve as a kind of temporary and safe, autonomous organizational testbed, wherein agreements can be negotiated with participants from other disciplines and functions to embrace a new practice over the course of a well-planned effort. Figure 9 shows the progression of new process development in the course of the case study project.

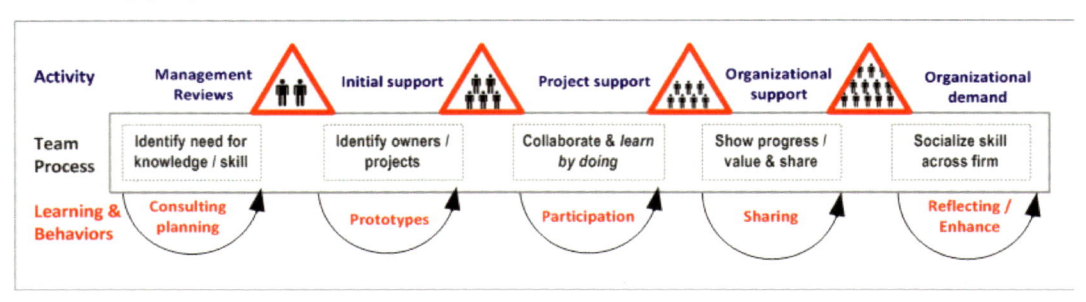

Figure 9. Iterative cycles of socialization and management review.

Socialization proceeds by careful coordination of project actions, internal learning, reflection and guidance, and explicit management support. Reviewing the socialization process in the abstract of Figure 9, we can identify team and organizational actions as they occur over the timeline of a given project. The activities in each iteration include team processes and new learning and behaviors associated with the process. At the conclusion of each iteration we show a management review or organizational milestone before continuing to the next activity. These activities are indicative of the progression of a socialization effort in a project context, but are not meant to be definitive.

The project team's process starts with the identification of need and ends with socializing skills to meet organizational demand. The central effort is to locate and engage an appropriate project that requires the skills and products from socialized practices. At the conclusion of each team iteration, an organizational diagnostic or meeting (triangle) is sought to expand scope for the unfolding process.

Usually an organization will have selected a critical project, and the consulting proposal may be used as the initial plan. This plan should be reconfigured by team co-creation, followed by a management review. Each triangle also represents a significant encounter or meeting where team members reported progress and requested support. Management support was crucial for publicizing the value of the project, drawing attention to the importance of the new skill practice, and encouraging its uptake in other projects.

The learning and behavior cycles (below the boxes) show a cyclic development of skills and processes for the project, including co-design of prototypes and materials, learning from designing concepts, user testing of prototypes, developing reports, tools for participation, and organizational presentations.

None of these activities recommend or argue against a product development or project management approach. This descriptive view of the diffusion of a given process shows how socialization gathers credibility through small steps, and accrues organizational endorsement by a combination of cross-disciplinary participation and official management support. It is planned like any other organizational project or intervention, and yet it simultaneously deploys *both* project deliverables (such as prototypes and product requirements) and the artifacts and skills associated with a new organizational process (e.g., user experience process).

CO-CREATING AN ITERATIVE ORGANIZATION

Most knowledge work, in any firm, should be structured for numerous brief iterative cycles between start and delivery. Individual skill development requires multiple occasions for trial and error, each followed by brief periods of feedback and improvement. Process development (the integration of methods and tools into a coherent repeatable practice) also requires iterative deployment, similar in principle to Agile software development. Several of the 12 Agile Manifesto principles (agilemanifesto.org) speak directly to the values of iterative process that enable deployment of any knowledge practice:

- Build projects around motivated individuals. Give them the environment and support they need, and trust them to get the job done.
- The best architectures, requirements, and designs emerge from self-organizing teams.
- At regular intervals, the team reflects on how to become more effective, then tunes and adjusts its behavior accordingly.

User experience and R&D practices especially are conducted as highly iterative workflows, translating knowledge between user research, representations of users, and design artifacts such as sketches and prototypes. Business requirements should be iterated (see Agile), not frozen, and then assessed in different ways by real customers. Allowance for failures and learning is accommodated with iterative processes, since subsequent cycles are available to revise plans, change variables and to assess responses and learning. If a product plan budgets for only a single validating (summative) usability test, the team has one chance to learn and improve the design. Due to the extreme pressures for completion and delivery, single-shot user research sessions tend to be engineered as *validation* sessions. Only serious functional issues are surfaced for change, and all ambiguity tends to be driven from the assessment. Unfortunately, we only observe what we prepare to find. If we narrow the scope of testing to validating the completeness and operation of functional requirements, we shut off opportunities for discovery.

Practices and processes are repeated and improved over time. However, organizations are not flexible with respect to failure. Many are internally competitive and defensive networks of people working within hierarchical structures, often with multiple conflicting agendas. Our challenge is to literally create more *recourse* in organizational processes, to iterate and learn from trial and error.

Learning from the informed worlds of Agile and user experience, we might consider creating better "organizational user experiences." We can turn the instruments and methods of design thinking to collaborate toward the betterment of organizational life, everyday work practices, messages and communications, and the internal deliverables that express ideas and proposals. We might also improve the "ease of use of business strategy." Many systemic problems I observe in larger organizations can be traced to communicating, organizing around, and translating from business strategy to operational decisions. Consider the communications path of a new strategic roadmap developed in executive conferences. The traditional means of communicating the critical changes to an organization's direction and goals are oral presentations, brief reports, and presentations. In the increasing complexity of today's work environment, these instruments fail to match the richness necessary for understanding and action. The iterative organization should be reframing the given business strategy in clear visual representations – a visual story, not just a roadmap. Understanding and agreement across the organization (otherwise known as alignment) become possible when members are able to visually comprehend the major goals of strategy. In a visual strategic plan, people can readily assess the industry position, expected changes in the marketplace, and the formulation or elimination of products and services in concert with the strategy.

Socializing Strategic Communications

Organizational transformation and strategy will benefit significantly from a socialization approach, as these are knowledge translation problems with a high cost of failure. Practically speaking, traditional strategy rollouts incur a significant friction of translation and loss of signal, meaning, and commitment. In the attempt to refine a single perspective from among multiple corporate contributors, meaning and original intent may be diminished. Most strategic designs are delivered as verbal reports, with poorly rendered statistical graphs. A comprehensive visual enhancement would greatly improve the organizational understanding of the shared journey ahead.

A dialogic communications style should be encouraged to facilitate the design and deployment of business and corporate strategy. Progressive organizations allowing for inclusive participation will find authentic uptake and ownership of the concepts and proposals. Dialogue will generate commitment in the excitement spurred by the very act of sharing and listening to matters of concern. By providing for iterations of the strategy during its design, participants will realize their contributions may make a difference. Management is relieved of much of the burden of "getting it right the first time."

We should follow our own observations and learning of the organization as a system of internal users. Within this recursive system (in which we all participate as users), we can start by moving observations up the circle of empathy (or the management hierarchy if you will).

Managers do care about the organization and their shared goals. Our challenge here is to learn and perform from double-loop learning ourselves, addressing root causes and "governing variables" of issues we encounter in organizational user research. We do this by systematic reflection on patterns, and improving processes incrementally, and not just "fixing things" (single-loop learning). The socialization process was designed to accomplish this risk-mitigating iteration when instantiating new practices in an organization. This perspective toward organizational participation, learning, and action will become a powerful metaphor for managing in successful firms in this century.

Socialization as a Leadership Perspective

The socialization approach originally intended to manage three problems. We needed rapid organizational deployment of available skills for a rapid turnaround design project. We needed to share authority across organizational boundaries to marshal resources and gain acceptance for the product design. We needed to establish a new set of practices in a short period of time that would be sustainable after the consulting engagement ended. At the time, it was not apparent this approach could be considered a leadership style. Each of the parties in the design project team served as a thought and practice leader within their own department, and each was supported in turn by their managers, and given wide latitude.

In the course of deployment of a socialization process for a user experience practice in a large organization we discovered its effectiveness for addressing several root causes of organizational failure. It accomplished the following:

- Socialization healed poor (isolated and constrained) communications across departments and in the hierarchy.
- It surpassed expectations and obviated the need for imported and brittle "best practices."
- It replaced the ineffective habits of identifying and attending to user concerns.
- It introduced sufficient cycle time to circulate learning and to repair discovered defects and issues.

Traditional approaches to process management (business re-engineering) and institutionalization ignore the power of socialized communications networks and currently effective practices existing in the firm. A competitive corporate culture creates an environment of internal competition, preventing managers from recognizing and accepting the validity of these often "homegrown" skill bases as significant resources. A top-down institutionalization effort often insists on a clean slate orientation to process creation, where (supposedly) marginal practices are replaced by endorsed, canonical methods and formal skill training. Socialization, instead, seeks out and appropriates such marginal practices as inherently valuable expressions of developing skill and commitment. People who have developed skills learned on their own initiative are usually willing to donate personal time and commitment to new efforts requiring their contribution, especially when the invitation extends from peer relationships. Socialization adapts new methods as they are learned and adapted to existing practices as an organizational template upon which to attach the new skills.

People working in marginalized departments have little incentive to contribute to a top-down institutional reorganization. They are often forced to continually reposition themselves and maintain perceived viability in a competitive culture. An observation from the case study shows that "old hands" in an organization, often experts in established practices, recognize that externally imported processes often fail, and may tacitly withhold commitment. After all, "old hands" in any older firm may have survived many other reorganizations by establishing a personal and persistent knowledge base, their own non-appropriable organizational knowledge.

Our experience with socialization indicates that locally innovated, invented-here processes are readily embraced by long-term employees. If any conflicts should be noted, it is with managers who champion an externally-developed process they wish to import or adapt to the organization themselves. It is doubtful that an externally-designed process or its deliverables could be successfully adapted to a socialization approach. Proponents of adapting a known approach from another firm or industry might evaluate the needs for practices and deliverables, and adapt the new practice to produce the desired materials (prototypes, research, visual communication artifacts), while remaining cautious about the value of employing an external process of any kind. It is not a short cut to performance.

Figure 10 compares the dynamics of the socialization process with institutionalization. Both can be seen as a series of actions within networks, with the biggest differences in the direction (arrows) and relationships between leadership and responsibility in the organization at large.

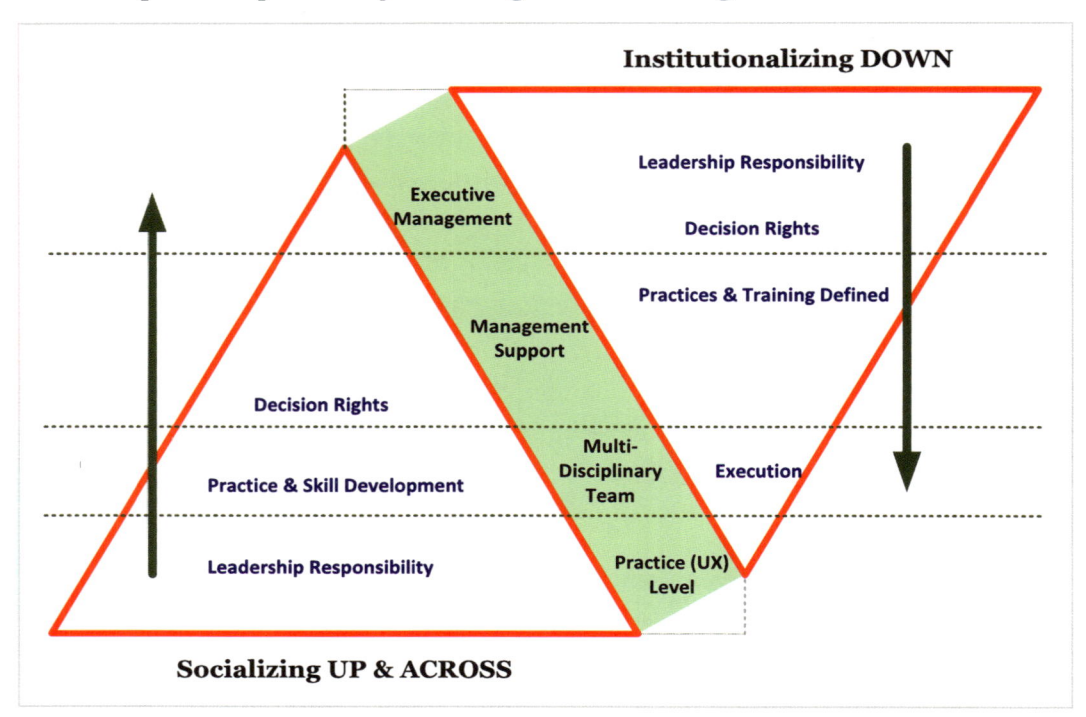

Figure 10. Socialization draws leadership up from the practice.

Socialization is led from the practice level, up the hierarchy (gaining management support) and across the multiple teams and departments needed to support the project with resources and committed individuals. Skill development and training follows the actual project requirements, some planned and some skills taught "just in time" to build competency progressively. Institutionalization normally identifies a set of necessary skills and trains groups of people in advance of their application. Finally, decision rights are earned by individuals demonstrating leadership and are given by the very pragmatic needs of the project. Leadership may be held by a project leader, or diffused across team members, but the socialization style negotiates a defined scope for autonomous decision making based on the project plan and its attendant needs for resources and practice development.

All organizations institutionalize their business processes, and over time we expect the socialized user experience practices in the case study to be formalized, documented, managed, and repeated continually. Once they are learned and refined, they become what business theorists call organizational routines, "generative systems that produce recognizable, repetitive patterns of interdependent actions," (Pentland and Feldman, 2008). Routines are considered the means by which knowledge becomes socialized and collectively known and shared within an organization. Collective knowledge in organizational routines embeds deep know-how into the coordination of work, creating context-specific practices that cannot be appropriated by competitors, or by individuals that leave the firm. A firm's strategic knowledge capabilities are developed in collective practices, which "embedded in the form of routines and operating procedures, allowed for the possibility that the collective had knowledge which is unknown to any of its members" (Nelson and Winter, 1982).

Organizational routines generate "net new" knowledge, and are mechanisms by which explicit knowing is internalized (to tacit) and reconfigured into everyday operations. This process is not typically considered a function of leadership. The socialization approach shows that a bottom-up, interdependent leadership role makes a difference, that processes are not merely introduced and taken up passively. Pentland's research suggests organic practices developed in response to an innovation need, such as Marketline's user experience functions, should be designed with narrative actions, adapting actions to networks and creating new networks. He argues against traditional design *methodologies* that only lead to formation of artifacts. Instead, effective routines establish a process for knowledge creation and continual learning, which may manifest in many new types of artifacts necessary in the context of creative applications.

Many organizational practices, and especially design, user experience, and engineering, establish methods for producing internal artifacts that document the outcomes of work, of participatory sessions, and artifacts such as prototypes and user videos. These critical communications tools are necessary for sharing results and demonstrating the effectiveness of the practice. However, these should be considered provisional and often interim outputs of a dynamic process. They reflect the composition of ideas and knowledge contributed in the project, and should be created more for the purposes of effective communication, and not specifically "design" uses that designers or engineers will adopt directly. When new practices are being socialized, understanding is more important than direct utility and immediate application. Allowance for gaps and incomplete knowledge in prepared materials, user representations, and designs encourages participation and collaboration. Group sensemaking is facilitated when the different disciplines working together can come to a common understanding and determine a joint course of action.

Socialization affirms that a longer-term, better understood, and organizationally resilient adoption of a process occurs when people in peripheral roles learn the practices through participation and gradual progression of sophistication. The practices employed in a socialization approach are nearly the opposite (in temporal order) of the institutionalization approach:

1. Find a significant need among projects (e.g., to understand and design for user experience) and bring rapid, lightweight methods to solve obvious problems.
2. Have management present the early successes and lessons learned.
3. Refrain from assigning management to the new practice area; lateral roles should come to accept and integrate the value first.
4. Identify the same needs and applications in other projects. Establish an informal internal consulting function and provide tactical services with available time as much as possible.
5. Develop skills, tools, and practices within the scope of *product* needs. Engage customers in field and document requirements and user representations in full participation with other roles on the product team.

6. Build an organic demand and interest in the new practice. Provide consulting and advice to other projects as capability expands.
7. Collaborate with product line managers and business owners to adapt and develop meaningful interim products useful to their decision making and development needs. (For example, integrate usability interview and personas into requirements and project management.)
8. Determine lifecycle decision points and match outputs to decisions.
9. Establish the new practice area as a stable routine and as a managed organizational function over a period of months, not weeks.
10. Provide awareness training, discussion sessions, and formal education as necessary to support and draw resources to the practice.
11. Continue with assessments and process renewal, staffing, and building competency as routines are established.

In socialization, failure *is* an option. In the everyday actions of learning and navigating the organization, leaders need latitude to explore, experiment, dialogue, learn, and adapt by trial and error. Things will not be done perfectly, but rather, done transparently and sincerely with a primary goal of learning and adapting to what works. We should be creating *more* opportunities to allow for observable failure points and process breakdowns. Facilitate multidisciplinary requirements reviews to challenge the fit to user needs. Organize a roundtable evaluation as a dialogue process, bringing marginalized perspectives on board, such as customer service, to review developing product concepts and prototypes. Create opportunities and articulate the double-loop learning points, such as:

"Yes, we'll fix the design, but our process for reporting user feedback limits us to tactical fixes. Let's dig further into the implications of the user feedback and then share what we've learned with management in one week."

We can create these opportunities by looking for issues and presenting them in simple cooperative terms, such as market dynamics, competitive landscape, feature priority (and overload), and user adoption. This will take time and patience, but then, its recursive. In the end we'll have made our case without major confrontations.

CONCLUSIONS

At a major user experience conference, Intuit's founder Scott Cook famously said: "The best we can hope to bat is .500. If you're getting better than that, you're not swinging for the fences. Even Barry Bonds, steroids or not, is not getting that. We need to celebrate failure."

Intelligent managers recognize and even celebrate failures as part of the game. How else will we learn and improve? If we are NOT failing at anything, how do we even know that we're trying? Our cultural problem is recognizing when failure is indeed an option, and how to sell that value of failures and breakdowns when it goes against the strong need to "win" in most corporate worlds.

A problem with socially-enabled organizational failures is the lack of early warning communications allowable in the human network. Consider the explicit warnings given to financial firms before their total operational failures in 2008. As always in "social systems" problems, a paradox shows up: How can an event so spectacular in its impact be so difficult to observe when in progress? Why are the very stakeholders eventually responsible for the failure the least likely to pay attention to the problem? Why do we organize our projects and systems so that priorities are so hard to change, we assume enormous risk and hope for the best?

We have outlined a clear value proposition for allowing failure and encouraging dialogue when it happens. Perhaps the best argument is that finding and fixing small failures on an ongoing basis prevents large-scale failures that occur later when we ignore reality.

Small failures are overlooked or swept aside when teams choose to value the instrumental (efficiency, progress, getting the job done) and trade off aspects of quality (usability, fit to user's work, total experience). Furthermore, early design decisions are compounded as these decisions determine platform architectures, which constrain and restrict the scope of later design decisions, and so on through the lifecycle of development. Micro-failures due to breakdowns in communications and loss of situation awareness continually occur and should be treated as everyday and normal. Breakdowns caught early in their impact lifecycle are opportunities already resolved.

Finally, consider an overriding philosophical issue in closing. Failure is perceived as a *purely* negative option in organizations that value and encourage the constant framing of individual work performance as "successful." The issue organizational leaders should address is their own framing of what constitutes successful and rewarded action. People are promoted for short-term wins, not for daring risks that end in big flops. As suggested by Scott Cook, organizational success requires the risk-taking that leads to strike-outs. Players must be rewarded for playing "full out," and for playing the game of communication well. When individuals are led to believe that every action and statement must be perceived as successful, personal and organizational failures will never be recognized as learning opportunities or teachable moments.

There are no neat, complete answers that sufficiently respond to the complicated, "wicked" problems found in every modern organization. Complex projects and situations require flexibility and generative thinking, including:

- *Both* leadership *and* the muddle of collaborative trial and error.
- Rapid analysis of root causes and interactions, based on quality data, the wisdom of experience, and thoughtful insight.
- Shared reflection about this rapid analysis (in dialogue) to synchronize views and perspectives from different stakes in the firm.
- The creation of strategies that include multiple options, not just a single planned, optimal solution.
- The freedom to autonomously negotiate plans and actions, and the allowance to respond to management and self-reflect on their impact.

We should expect decision makers to be continually overwhelmed, and we must find ways to simplify the available alternatives. They must narrow down a field of options in the course of action, deal with the cognitive load of massive volume of often-conflicting information (from multiple channels), organize consensus at the top, and communicate the choices to the organization at large. In crisis situations, leaders will not have the capacity and luxury of reflection and strategic foresight. A rapid, more continuous approach to organizational sensemaking is called for. Sensemaking (according to Weick's view mentioned previously) responds to attention-arousing situations, especially those with significant uncertainty. Communications will always fall short of actual knowledge, and people in the workplace tend to communicate only when deemed necessary.

So much of what is known about a situation is never shared, until a sensemaking event calls for it.

Sensemaking is literally "making common sense," generating a forward-thinking response based on shared perspectives about the critical factors sensed in the problem and the environment. People make sense of situations as they occur by conversation, as socially-organized responses in words and actions that generate a new context for further action and understanding. Sensemaking is what led to the socialization process, to designing approaches that best fit the ecological (organizational, systemic and local) needs of the firm and the marketplace. A *continuous* approach to sensemaking doesn't wait for a problem to manifest. People have powerful human skills of intuition, imagination, contextual memory, and curiosity that are dampened by disuse in organizational settings. With more acceptance of these styles of tacit knowing, teams can learn from the different perspectives available in a project and navigate the infinite shades of gray (and vast creative white space) between perfect success and disappointing failure.

In organizational reality, not all stories end as well as this narrative of the organizational recovery from market failure. As always in any story, case study or not, there were many twists and turns we specifically avoided revealing in this particular telling. In business, there are punch lines we tell only in private, but these do not change the meaning and learning gained from these experiences with organizational leadership. In any passionate team effort, failures or successes may occur, but are only made real in the telling. We'll end our telling of this story on such a note, allowing for the contribution of future narratives to our own learning journey.

Bibliography

Argyris, C. (1992). *On organizational learning.* London: Blackwell.

Argyris, C. and Schön, D. (1978). *Organizational learning. A theory of action perspective.* Reading, MA: Addison-Wesley.

Columbia Accident Investigation Board. (2003). Columbia *Accident Investigation Board Report Volume 1,* August 2003. Washington, DC: Columbia Accident Investigation Board.

Dweck, C. (2008). *Mindset: The new psychology of success.* New York: Ballantine.

Howard, R. (1992). The CEO as organizational architect: an interview with Xerox's Paul Allaire. *Harvard Business Review, 70* (5), 106-121.

Jones, P.H. (2008). Socialization of Practice in a Process World: Toward Participatory Organizations. *Participatory Design Conference 2008.* Bloomington, IN: Indiana University.

Jones, P.H. (2007). Socializing a knowledge strategy. In E. Abou-Zeid (Ed.) *Knowledge Management and Business Strategies: Theoretical Frameworks and Empirical Research,* pp. 134-164. Hershey, PA: Idea Group.

Jones, P.H. (2002). When successful products prevent strategic innovation. *Design Management Review, 13* (2), 30-37.

Latour, B. (2008). *A Cautious Prometheus? A Few Steps Toward a Philosophy of Design.* Meeting of the Design History Society, Falmouth, Cornwall, 3rd September, 2008.

Lave, J. and Wenger, E. (1991). *Situated learning: Legitimate peripheral participation.* Cambridge, UK: Cambridge University Press.

Nadler, D.A., Gerstein, M.S. and Shaw, R.B. (1992) *Organizational Architecture: Designs for changing organizations.* Jossey-Bass.

Nelson, R. & Winter, S. (1982). An evolutionary theory of economic change. Cambridge, MA: Harvard University Press.

Nonaka, I. (1994). A dynamic theory of organizational knowledge creation. *Organization Science*, 5, 14-37.

Pentland, B.T. and Feldman, M.S. (2008) Designing routines: On the folly of designing artifacts, while hoping for patterns of action. *Information and Organization*, 18 (14), 235-250.

Raynor, M.E. (2007) *The strategy paradox: Why committing to success leads to failure (and what to do about it)*. New York: Currency Doubleday.

Rittel, H.W.J. and Weber, M.W. (1973). Dilemmas in a general theory of planning. *Policy Sciences*, 4, 155-169.

Taleb, N.N (2007).*The Black Swan: The impact of the highly improbable.* New York: Random House.

Weick, W.E. (1995). *Sensemaking in Organizations.* London: Sage Publications

Weick, K.E. (2001). *Making Sense of the Organization.* New York: Blackwell Publishing.

LETTER FROM THE PUBLISHER

Dear Reader,

I first met Pete Jones almost ten years ago, when we both shared the same employer (not at the case study) for several years. I was newly involved in product management for our flagship product and Pete was in what was then called "Human Factors" leading the UI work for the company's #1 priority enhancement. To be frank, I found his high articulateness and assertiveness rather annoying! Like many product managers, I wanted the usability team to design something that did what I wanted it to do and looked good—but without a lot of backchat. (Sorry, Pete!)

To be fair, I always listened to and got along well with the usability team—I was fortunate enough to manage them for a brief period—but it was only after several years of experience in the product management role that I began truly to understand just how valuable design professionals like Pete can be. Reading this essay reminds me all over again just how important it is for the organization to be socialized to the strategic value of usability and design. Now, with beautiful and efficient user-centered design at the strategic heart of many of the most successful companies in the world, Pete's message is more important, and more accurate, than ever. I'm proud to publish it.

—Fred Zimmerman, Nimble Books LLC,
Ann Arbor, Michigan, USA, 2008